Truth in Context

Truth in Context
An Essay on Pluralism and Objectivity

Michael P. Lynch

A Bradford Book
The MIT Press
Cambridge, Massachusetts
London, England

This book was set in Sabon on Miles 33 by Achorn Graphic Services, Inc., and was printed and bound in the United States of America.

First printing, 1998.

Library of Congress Cataloging-in-Publication Data

Lynch, Michael P. (Michael Patrick), 1966–
    Truth in context : an essay on pluralism and objectivity / Michael P. Lynch.
        p.   cm.
    "A Bradford book."
    Includes bibliographical references and index.
    ISBN 0-262-12212-X (hardcover : alk. paper)
    1. Truth. 2. Pluralism. 3. Objectivity. I. Title.
BD171.L87   1998
121—dc21   98-18000
                                                                      CIP

For Terry B., who put things in context in the first place

Contents

Preface

I first became interested in questions about truth and objectivity during an undergraduate year spent studying philosophy at the University of Glasgow. My intuitive belief then was that there could be more than one true account of some subject matter without that implying that every account is true. I still have that belief today, and I am even more convinced now that any sane human philosophy must account for this fact. This book is an attempt to sketch just such a philosophy—a view that allows for both realism about truth and pluralism about the world.

Philosophers generally have pretensions to populism, and I am no exception, but questions about truth and relativism are undoubtedly in the foreground of contemporary intellectual culture. Such questions are faced in literary criticism, history, and the sciences as much as they are in philosophy. So while this is undoubtedly a book in the area of "analytic" metaphysics and epistemology, my motivation for writing it was not simply the abstract pursuit of truth in those fields. My motivation was to clear conceptual space for a more general dialogue on how to reconcile pluralism and objectivity. Accordingly, I have tried to define technical terms and have confined more esoteric remarks to the notes. Even so, the reader less familiar with technical philosophy may find it useful to skip certain sections initially (e.g., 1.5, 4.2, and the latter half of 5.5), returning to them after having gained an overall understanding of my argument.

Many people have helped me find my way through this complex maze of ideas. First thanks go to William Alston, who deftly supervised my first fumbling attempts at understanding truth and whose own work has deeply influenced my thinking on these and many other matters. Alston was also kind enough to provide extensive comments on a late draft of this book, which helped improve the text immeasurably. Mark Timmons, John Tienson, David Henderson, and Terence Horgan read an early version of the manuscript and met to discuss it with me over several weeks in the summer of 1997. I learned a huge amount during these sessions, and a much better book emerged as a result. Horgan, in particular, provided crucial advice and encouragement at every turn. Paul Bloomfield was kind enough to lend his services as a hardened realist and provided exhaustive commentary on the manuscript, helping me to avoid numerous mistakes. His support and friendship throughout have been invaluable. Special thanks go to my graduate and undergraduate students during the last two years, especially the participants in two seminars on truth and objectivity that I gave in the spring of 1996 and 1998. The first of these was where I initially tested many of my ideas on these subjects; the second helped to refine my presentation of them. Numerous others also provided helpful comments and conversations, including William Lawhead, John Post, Robert Neustadt, Ken Sufka, Michael Wakoff, John Hawthorne, R. M. Sainsbury, Alessandra Tanesini, Robert Westmoreland, Jennifer Case, José Benardete, Andrew Cortens, Hunter Hatfield, Karsten Steuber, Dave Truncellito, Howard Hewitt, and Terry Berthelot. To all the above, I express my thanks. What truth there is in what follows I share with them; the mistakes are my own.

Portions of chapter 2 are based on material that originally appeared under the title "Three Models of Conceptual Schemes" in *Inquiry* 40 (1998), no. 4. I am grateful to the University of Mississippi's Office of Research for providing me with much needed Summer Research Grants for 1996 and 1997, and to my chair, Michael Harrington, for providing an excellent environment in which to work.

Finally, I thank my parents and older siblings for inspiration. Artists all, it is they who taught me to see.

May 1998

Truth in Context

Introduction

Up to about 1850 almost everyone believed that sciences expressed truths that were exact copies of a definite code of non-human realities. But the enormously rapid multiplication of theories these latter days has well-nigh upset the notion of any one of them being a more literally objective kind of thing than another. There are so many geometries, so many logics, so many physical and chemical hypotheses, so many classifications, each one of them good for so much and yet not good for everything, that the notion that even the truest formula may be a human device and not a literal transcript has dawned upon us.

William James

The idea that was dawning on William James and other philosophers at the beginning of this century is no longer novel as we approach its end. The notion of *pluralism* shines brightly within academia and throughout the culture at large. In its most general form, pluralism is the idea that there can be more than one true story of the world; there can be incompatible, but equally acceptable, accounts of some subject matter. There are no absolute facts but a diversity of truths, all of which equally clamor for our attention. Once a subject of discussion only in philosophy, variations on this theme have found their way into the disciplines of psychology, physics, history, and educational theory, to name just a few. Yet the many problems involved in trying to understand pluralism, the problems that so vexed James and his critics, remain. Chief among them is the problem of finding room for objectivity inside the pluralist's picture of the world; it is the problem of allowing for *different* truths without slipping into the nihilistic position that there is no truth at all. Pluralists, like overly permissive parents, always seem on the brink of allowing anything to be true—of saying that anything goes. Finding a solution to the problem of how to reconcile pluralist philosophies with an objective notion of truth remains as the most pressing and difficult of the problems associated with such views.

Almost all of us assume in our everyday lives that pluralism and objectivity are compatible. In contemporary educational practice, for example, it is widely agreed that there is no one right way to teach a class, yet there are definitely wrong ways to do so, as many of us know from experience. We also tend to believe that there is no one best way to raise children, or to demonstrate romantic love for another, or to prepare a curry, although, again, there are mistaken ways of doing all these things. In our day-to-day lives, we find it natural and reasonable to assume that there can be a variety of equally good viewpoints, without feeling obliged to state that there must be a *best* viewpoint. It is as if (to use a simple analogy) we think there can be multiple winners despite the fact that there can be definite losers.

Yet even a little philosophical reflection dashes cold water on our intuitive conjunction of pluralism and objectivity when we try to extend it across the board. To begin with, the examples I have cited, while appealing, are examples involving actions and feelings. It is easy for most people to imagine more than one "right" way to act or feel in a particular situation. It is more difficult to understand how competing *descriptions of reality* could both be true. When we say that there could be more than one true account of the facts and yet that some accounts are mistaken, we seem to be trying to state the impossible. First, we seem to be saying that reality is *not* absolute, that there can be irreconcilable but equally true perspectives on the world; and second, that truth *is* absolute, that some perspectives are simply true, others are simply false. Many of the thinkers who reflect on this subject conclude that, in the descriptive sphere at least, pluralism and objectivity are inconsistent with one another. Such pessimism is not restricted to one particular side of the academic fence. It can be found, for example, on both sides of the increasingly shrill debate over the objectivity of knowledge and science. In the name of "postmodernism," "historicism," and "antirealism," one side of the debate declares that we must embrace relativism and deems any talk of objective truth as philosophically naive. The opposition, invoking "realism" and "common sense," argues that *any* relativism leads to nihilism. There is objective truth, these theorists hold, and this means that there can be one and only one true story of the world. Both sides would appear to agree on one thing only: You can't have it both ways. Either there are different but equally true perspectives on the world and hence truth is not objective, or truth is objective and there can be but one true perspective on the world. There is no middle path.

This book argues that there is a middle path: a thoroughgoing metaphysical pluralism is compatible with realism about truth. In the game of knowledge and opinion, there may be multiple winners, but there are also definite losers. One can be a pluralist without having to believe that anything goes.

Metaphysical pluralism is *pluralist* because it implies that true propositions and facts are relative to conceptual schemes or worldviews; it is *metaphysical* because the facts in question concern the nature of reality— facts about God, mind, and the universe. Realism about truth, on the other hand, is the view that a proposition is true just when the world is as that proposition says it is. Truth, on a realist view like the correspondence theory, is a relation between the world and our thought, irreducible to epistemic concepts of justification or warrant—even justification or warrant in the long run or at the "ideal limit." Philosophers generally assume that these two views are opposites: if the facts are soft, so must be truth. In arguing otherwise, my objective is to point out that we can avoid what Putnam has called the "recoil phenomenon"—the process by which philosophers bounce back and forth from an extreme absolutism and an equally extreme relativism.[1] The difficulty lies not in persuading people to take this middle path—for I think that many of us who are not prisoners of theory do believe that a middle way is possible—but in explaining *how* it is possible.

The compatibility of pluralism and objectivity is not only of academic interest. The problem of how to incorporate multiple viewpoints into one culture (or one culture into multiple viewpoints) is one of the most important political issues of our age. Metaphysics, as Kant knew, is important because it can help us understand the limits and structure of our moral and political problems and, to that degree, help us see our way through to a solution to those problems. As I shall argue, the ubiquity of metaphysical concepts ensures that a pluralism concerned with such concepts has wider implications. Thus, getting straight on how metaphysical pluralism can be objective will hopefully allow us to make the same claims for pluralism in the normative realm.

But the immediate goal of this book is limited to showing that metaphysical pluralism and realism about truth are compatible. The first and most formidable task is to elucidate a plausible form of metaphysical pluralism. This must be done in the face of damning objections to the effect that the view is incoherent or, worse, simply trivial. Presenting a coherent metaphysical pluralism, and answering these objections, is the subject of the first four chapters. Chapter 1 introduces the debate and the main principles of metaphysical pluralism, according to which the contents of our thought and the very facts that such thought can express are intrinsically relative to one among many conceptual schemes. Chapter 2 looks into what a pluralist could mean by "conceptual scheme" and presents a new theory of the notion. In chapter 3, I argue that, understood properly, the pluralist doctrine of content-relativity presupposes the Wittgensteinian theme (also echoed in Putnam) that certain of our concepts—including concepts like *object*, *fact*, and *existence*—are indeterminate and open to being radically extended in new and unforeseen directions. For the pluralist, our most basic metaphysical concepts are *fluid*. Chapter 4 develops this theme in a way that allows the pluralist to answer some of the more troublesome objections to her view.

After I have sketched a coherent version of metaphysical pluralism, the next task before me is to explain and motivate realism about truth and to show how conjoining it with pluralism makes for an intelligible philosophical position in its own right. Chapter 5 discusses the two main theories of truth that pluralists have typically adopted in the past and argues that neither is particularly well suited for pluralism. Drawing on Alston's minimal realism about truth, as well as some suggestive remarks of Crispin Wright's, I spend the rest of the chapter developing a position that is at once realist and pluralist about truth. Chapter 6 concludes the book by answering a number of objections and logical paradoxes that face any combination of pluralism and realism.

This overall position, the result of combining pluralism and alethic realism, I call *relativistic Kantianism*—a term I first heard used by William Alston in relation to Hilary Putnam's view in *Reason, Truth, and History*

(1981). This essay is very much influenced by Putnam's work in the last two decades. In fact, the pluralism I develop is deeply based on Putnam's own views. Yet what *I* call relativistic Kantianism is importantly distinct from his pragmatic realism. Most crucially, Putnam has denied that metaphysical pluralism (which he often refers to as "conceptual relativity") is consistent with a realist view of truth. It is precisely this denial that I aim to undermine. Furthermore, relativistic Kantianism, unsurprisingly, is more Kantian than Putnam's own position. To cite only one point, I argue that the pluralist metaphysician has nothing to fear from admitting the existence of what Putnam has derisively called THE WORLD and what Kant called the noumenal realm.

Throughout, I am concerned with showing that relativistic Kantianism is a viable philosophical position, one which makes a certain amount of sense, hangs together, is internally consistent, and is nontrivial. I am much less concerned to prove, via attacks on absolutism, that relativistic Kantianism must be true. Besides running counter to the spirit of the view itself, that is simply another project. One might be tempted to say that my focus is therefore defense, not offense, but in the end that distinction is too arbitrary to be of much use. Given the troublesome objections that face epistemic views of truth, showing that pluralism is compatible with *alethic* realism (realism about truth) is itself a vindication of pluralist metaphysics. Further, I argue that there is a connection between pluralism at the conceptual level and pluralism at the metaphysical level—an important fact since so many philosophers see pluralism about concepts as plausible. And, of course, one provides indirect support for a position by addressing and solving outstanding objections.

In the remaining pages of this introduction I would like briefly to touch upon two terminological issues not mentioned in the main body of the text. These points will be of interest primarily to the specialist; I urge those less interested in purely technical issues to skip ahead to chapter 1.

First, some readers may be puzzled as to why I am using the terms "pluralism" and "absolutism" rather than the more familiar "realism" and "antirealism." There are two reasons for this terminological decision. Most obviously, I need the realist/antirealist contrast for my discussion of differing conceptions on truth, and it seems best not to spread these words around too much. Moreover, while I am fairly confident that my use of "realism" *with regard to truth* accords with how it is used in the literature on that particular subject, I am less sure that there is any common way of making the distinction between realism and antirealism *in general*. For instance, philosophers often use the word "antirealist" to cover positions as disparate as nominalism, idealism, and Dummettian verificationism. Some might label what I'm calling metaphysical pluralism as a general antirealism, but given that word's wide variety of uses and given that many of the other views often labeled "antirealist" will turn out (as we shall see) to be absolutist in my sense, I think it best to use another set of terms entirely.

Second, the word "pluralism," like any popular philosophical term, is unfortunately associated with a bewildering variety of positions on any number of topics. One can be a pluralist about education, history, morals, religion, scientific knowledge, or, as in the present case, metaphysics. But even when I stipulate that the field of interest is facts about what ultimately exists, I face ambiguity in the term. The chief problem is that there are several continua along which one can be a pluralist with regard to facts. In particular, we need to distinguish between *vertical* and *horizontal pluralism*.[2] Vertical pluralism is the view that there is more than one type of fact to be had in the world, and hence that different "levels" of fact-stating discourse may not be reducible to a more basic discourse. Vertical pluralism is radically nonreductivist about facts. The vertical pluralist, for instance, sees no reason to attempt a reduction of all facts to physical facts but rather holds that facts about, e.g., the mind, art, and morality hold an equal claim to ontological primacy.[3]

Horizontal pluralism, on the other hand, holds that there can be incompatible facts within a single level of discourse. Hence, a horizontal pluralist might hold that there can be incompatible but equally correct moral facts or physical facts or facts about the nature of the mind. Typically, this is described by saying that the facts in question are "relative" to worldviews, conceptual schemes, or the like. When I argue that metaphysical pluralism is compatible with realism about truth, this is the sort of pluralism I have in mind.

The logical relationship between different types of pluralism is complex. A vertical pluralist, someone who believes (for instance) that facts about morality can't be reduced to facts about physics, might still deny that there could be incompatible moral facts. Simply because you think that moral facts are autonomous from physical facts doesn't mean that you think that moral facts are relative. So vertical pluralism about facts of a certain type doesn't imply horizontal pluralism about facts of that type. The situation involving the converse, however, is more complicated. To get straight on this, we need another distinction: that between *global* and *local* forms of horizontal pluralism. A local pluralist restricts her view to a particular type of fact or discourse, such as moral facts. So a local horizontal pluralist about morality would believe that there are incompatible moral facts, while a local vertical pluralist about morality would believe that moral facts are not reducible to another set of facts. A global horizontal pluralism, on the other hand, is pluralism with regard to every type of fact; pick any type of fact you wish, there can be incompatible but equally correct truths of that type. And global vertical pluralism is the view that no type of facts reduces to any other type of facts.

With this distinction in hand, we may now ask whether a local horizontal pluralism entails a local vertical pluralism. Let us take moral facts as the example. Does horizontal moral pluralism entail vertical moral pluralism? The question, in other words, concerns whether moral relativism implies that the (relative) moral facts are irreducible to physical facts. To say that one type of facts is reducible to another type of facts is to imply that the former can be completely explained in terms of the latter. But once moral facts are relativized to cultures or practices, then it seems that no set of physical facts alone will be able to capture or explain what is the case at the moral level. For any explanation of the moral facts would have to appeal to the culture or practice those facts were relative to. Relative moral facts, then, would seem irreducible to underlying physical facts, and hence local horizontal pluralism would appear to imply vertical pluralism.

The situation is even simpler when we ask whether global horizontal pluralism entails global vertical pluralism. Suppose that every fact is relative. If so, then any hostility toward pluralism along the vertical dimension would only be so much bluff. If there are no absolute facts, then there are no absolute facts about reducibility either, and hence, practically speaking, facts at different levels are autonomous. For all intents and purposes, a global horizontal pluralism ushers in global vertical pluralism as well.

In the terms of these distinctions, my focus is on a horizontal *metaphysical* pluralism, the view that there can be incompatible metaphysical facts. This is practically warranted as it allows me to deal with one of the more popular types of pluralism in contemporary philosophy. More important, metaphysical issues have pervasive consequences. As I argue throughout the book, metaphysical concepts and truths are interwoven into the fabric of our conceptual schemes at a very basic level. Thus if there is a plurality of metaphysical facts, facts about ultimate reality, then prima facie, at least, there could be a plurality of any sort of fact. Metaphysical pluralism plausibly implies global pluralism; in short, the metaphysical pluralist acts locally while thinking globally.

1

The Faces of Pluralism

Our life is an apprenticeship to the truth that around every circle another can be drawn; that there is no end in nature, but every end is a beginning; that there is always another dawn risen on mid-noon, and under every deep a lower deep opens.

Emerson

1.1 The Problem

Metaphysics is often defined as the search for the ultimate truth about reality. This definition reflects an ambiguity within metaphysics itself, for truths can be "ultimate" in two senses. They can be ultimate by being basic and fundamental—first principles; or they can be ultimate in that they take us beyond the appearances—beyond human misconceptions, prejudices, and frailties to the real nature of the world.

It is in this second sense that metaphysics is said to be capable of bringing us into contact with *absolute* truths. Just what these truths may be is a matter of debate, but regardless of whether the world is entirely material or immaterial, in perpetual change or constantly static, composed of many substances or just one, the traditional metaphysician believes that there is a single absolute nature of reality—the way the world is in itself. In short, there is a significant strain of *absolutism* in metaphysics. Metaphysical absolutism is the view, as William James once put it, that reality "stands ready-made and complete," leaving our intellects to "supervene with the one simple duty of describing it as it is already" (1910, 123). It is the idea that there are absolute facts about ultimate reality, facts that are as they are independently of our conceptual contributions.

The durability of absolutism as a bedrock assumption of philosophical inquiry is due to its intuitive force. Most of us believe that there are at least some questions that have only one right answer. Once we clarify the meanings of the words by which a question is expressed, the answer is not up to us but rather is dictated by how the world is "in itself." Extend this intuition to the questions of metaphysics and we have not only the position of Aristotle, Leibniz, and Spinoza but also of Russell, Lewis, and Kripke. Contemporary metaphysicians, no less than their historical counterparts, see metaphysics as the attempt to discover the one true nature of the world. The only way to do that is by coming up with a theory, which, any ontologist would admit, probably won't be completely right. Yet, hypothetically at least, there is a theory waiting "out there" that *is* completely right, and the search for that theory is the point of metaphysical inquiry.

Medieval scholastics, for example, believed that the world was a divine artifact, its structure and contents products of God's will. The true theory of the world would be the one that most accurately represented that structure, the one that (perhaps literally!) reads the mind of God. In like fashion, many philosophers and scientists today believe that science in general, and physics in particular, will reveal to us the ultimate and unique structure of the universe. As the physicist Stephen Hawking remarks, "The eventual goal of science is to provide a single theory that describes the whole universe" (1988, 10). This is the view known as "materialism"—everything is a physical thing or composed of physical things.[1] If materialism is true, then a completely successful physical science will explain everything—not only quantum phenomena and a cure for AIDS but also consciousness and the abstract objects of mathematics. Of course, materialists typically do not believe that this unique physical structure of the world was divinely created, nor that discovering its nature is discovering divine intentions, but they do share two beliefs with their medieval counterparts: the world stands "ready-made," and, hypothetically at least, we can give one true account of the nature of that world.

Yet since the inception of metaphysics, absolutism has been balanced by the equally strong intuition that the world is tolerant of *more* than a single description of its nature. This is metaphysical pluralism, the idea that there can be more than one true metaphysic, that there can be a plurality of incompatible, but equally acceptable, conceptual schemes. These conceptual schemes are ways of dividing reality into objects and kinds of objects; they are ways of categorizing the world. The pluralist intuition is that the world does not dictate to us which of these ways of categorizing is the best, the most correct, or the way the world really is "in itself." The pluralist denies that there are any absolute facts about ultimate reality; the facts themselves reflect our conceptual points of view.

In its contemporary form, metaphysical pluralism has one of its roots in Kant, and in particular, in the Kantian insight that our knowledge of the world, and hence "the world as it is for us," is in some sense constructed.[2] For Kant, experience did not simply write on the blank slates of the mind. A person's conceptual scheme, what Kant would have called the "forms of intuition" and the "categories," shapes raw sensory experience into knowledge. On the Kantian view, to even perceive an object is to conceptualize experience in a certain way. And according to Kant, at least, this means that we cannot consider an object as it is independently of our conceptualizations. We can only consider objects as they appear to us. The result is a type of *internalism*: All thought and talk about the world is internal to our conceptual scheme. Your thought and experience is literally *in*formed by concepts, just as your visual field is structured and limited by your eyesight and position.

Kant, however, was no pluralist. For him, there was *one and only one* set of categorical and formal concepts, which together were the form of all possible experience. So if one of the roots of pluralism is the now familiar point that experience and thought is perspectival in character, a second is the idea that there can be more than one such perspective: there is no unique set of concepts we must use to think about the world.[3] Apply this intuition to our basic metaphysical concepts, and the result is metaphysical pluralism, according to which there can be more than one true account of ultimate reality.

A common reason for taking metaphysical pluralism seriously is the apparent intractability of metaphysical disputes. This is a familiar consideration in morality, art, and religion: it is often thought (rightly or wrongly) that there is no neutral ground from which to adjudicate moral, aesthetic, or religious disputes. Different views about what is good, beautiful, or sacred can be radically divergent, even logically inconsistent, and yet at the same time seem to fit the agreed-upon facts equally well. A familiar conclusion is that there is no objective basis for choosing between such perspectives, and therefore, that what is good, beautiful, or sacred is not absolute but relative to the perspectives themselves. The same intuitions can also find a grip in metaphysics. Most philosophers, even those who are absolutists, can remember feeling frustrated by the apparent intractability of one metaphysical debate or other. And certainly (as students of philosophy are continually reminding us) the "ordinary" person is often nonplussed by the underdetermination of metaphysical facts by the evidence. There just doesn't appear to be any objective way to resolve some metaphysical disputes. Take the debate between the global materialist and immaterialist. One says that the world is entirely material or physical; the other declares that it is entirely immaterial or nonphysical. If we assume that both views are internally consistent and that (as each theorist will allege) each is consistent with how the world appears to us, how are we to adjudicate the dispute? In the face of such underdetermination, the pluralist intuition is not to insist on the absolute truth of just one metaphysical view but to admit more than one answer to such questions.

The obvious problem with metaphysical pluralism is that it threatens a loss of objectivity. If there is a plurality of correct perspectives, it seems that we cannot say that any are mistaken. In short, the chief problem for pluralism is truth. If the facts are relative or internal to conceptual schemes, it would seem that truth must be as well. Surprisingly, there is widespread agreement between pluralists and absolutists on this point. Most pluralist philosophers implicitly or explicitly concede that metaphysical pluralism is incompatible with a realist theory of truth. *Realism* about truth is the view that a proposition is true just when the world is as that proposition says that it is. Truth is not a matter of what we think about the world but about the way the world is. Yet by claiming that facts about the nature of reality are relative in some way, the pluralist seems committed to an antirealism about truth. The metaphysical pluralist, it would appear, must believe that the concept of truth is either subjectively relative, as Richard Rorty and Nelson Goodman sometimes seem to think, or that truth is epistemic in character, as Hilary Putnam has argued.[4] Both the literature and common sense indicate that if the facts are soft, so too must be our concept of truth.[5]

The thesis of this book is that this assumption is mistaken. Metaphysical pluralism is compatible with a realist theory of truth. The upshot of combining these two views is a sort of *relativized Kantianism*, according to which all thought and fact is internal to one among a possible plurality of conceptual schemes, and yet truth is a relation between our thought and the world. Such a view denies that there can be a cosmic exile, God's-eye point of view, or Archimedean standpoint from which to state the one true story of the universe. My view is therefore antimetaphysical insofar as metaphysics is the search for ultimate, *absolute* truth. But truths can also be "ultimate" by being basic, and metaphysics can be seen as the search for, and creation of, these first principles. It is in this sense that relativistic Kantianism is itself a metaphysical view.

1.2   Faces of Absolutism

Metaphysical pluralism and absolutism are both two-faced. Each view has two aspects, the one representational, concerning propositional content, the other metaphysical, concerning fact. In short, absolutism is the view that there are absolute propositions and facts, and pluralism is the denial of both.

Bernard Williams implicitly illustrates the dual nature of absolutism when he says,

Reflecting on the world that is there *anyway*, independent of our experience, we must concentrate not in the first instance on what our beliefs are about, but on how they represent what they are about. We can select among our beliefs and features of our world picture some that we can reasonably claim to represent the world in a way to the maximum degree independent of our perspective and its peculiarities. (1985, 138–39)

The result is what Williams calls the "absolute conception of the world," which "might be arrived at by any investigators, even if they are very different from us" (1985, 138–139). His point is that ontological claims, claims that the world is some way "in itself," imply that the absolute conception of the world contains a description of the world being that way. For Williams, the notion of an absolute conception of the world gives substantive content to the idea of the world as it is in itself. Of course, Williams believes not that we currently possess such a conception, or even that we will ever have one, but only that there exists such a conception of the world in logical space, toward which our efforts at knowledge aim.

The implication is that there are two aspects of the absolutist view. Relying on a bit of technical jargon, I shall call the representational aspect of the view, *content absolutism*. The content of an assertion, utterance, or belief is *what* is asserted, uttered, or believed; it is the proposition expressed by that assertion.[6] Content absolutism is the view that what we say or think on some occasion—the proposition we express—is not relative to any worldview, perspective, or conceptual scheme. Now a natural way of individuating propositions is by their *truth-conditions*, the conditions in virtue of which they are true. So, to say that propositions are nonrelative is to say that the conditions in virtue of which they are true (or false) are determinate independently of the context, broadly conceived, in which they were expressed. We might say that propositions are absolute when the conditions under which they are true are *external* to any worldview or human perspective.

Here is an intuitive way of understanding what this means. Imagine a list of every true proposition in the entire universe—or at least the longest such list possible—including such unassuming propositions as *Water is a liquid*, *The desk is cluttered*, and *The Earth has one moon*. Content absolutism about this list would be the view that, as a matter of metaphysical necessity, the propositions on the list, save those about minds, perspectives, or those things uncontroversially dependent upon them, will have no intrinsic connection to any mind or perspective.[7] The list is consistent without any relativistic qualification or connection to conceptual perspectives or schemes. It is unique in that there can be no other list of true propositions that is not included within, or identical to, the original list.[8]

So content absolutism implies that at best there can be only one true account of some subject matter. Of course, the absolutist needn't believe that anyone (or any group, for that matter) has ever *considered* this account. Nor must she hold that the one true account of the world be given in only one language. Nor does absolutism require that the one list of true propositions be complete, which would fly in the face of certain logical paradoxes.[9] The key point is that content is absolute; propositions are determinate independently of perspectives or conceptual schemes.

The second aspect of the absolutist position I shall call *fact absolutism*. Again, the general idea here can be explained by appeal to the hypothetical totality of facts. According to fact absolutism, the totality of facts, should it exist, is necessarily unique and nonrelative. Facts are external to worldviews. Necessarily (in the strongest, most metaphysical sense of that word), there can be one and only one totality of facts; there is one and only one way the world is. As James says, the world comes "ready-made." I take a fact to be a way the world is, or what we might call an obtaining state of affairs. That is, lemons being sour, the actual state of affairs of lemons being sour, is one and the same thing as the fact that lemons are sour. But I offer no theory of either facts or states of affairs: I take absolutism to be consistent with whatever they turn out to be (abstract objects Russellian composite, spatially located objects, etc.)[10]

Fact and content absolutism are two sides of one view because each one naturally leads to the other. It is fairly obvious that content absolutism leads to an absolutism about fact. If there can only be one true account of the world, there must be only one way the world is. But the implication works the other way around as well: if there can be only one way the world is, then there can be only one true account of the world.

Let me spell this out. Instances of the following principle are clearly true a priori (where "*p*" stands for some proposition):

T-SCHEMA   *The proposition that p is true if, and only if, p.*

The two sides of the schema here are intuitively and necessarily connected. The proposition that grass is green *could not* be true if grass were not green, in virtue of what we mean by "true." And just as obviously, if it were false that grass is green, then grass would not, and could not, be green. In the same way, the following is also true a priori:

F-SCHEMA   *It is a fact that p if, and only if, p.*

Hence the following is also true a priori: the proposition that *p* is true if, and only if, it is a fact that *p*. Thus, together with the unique list of true propositions, there must also be a set or "list" of states of affairs, facts, or ways in which the world is. And if there is one unique way (or ways) in which the world is, then there will be a corresponding totality of true propositions. In particular, if one of the obtaining states of affairs is the state of affairs that minds are nonphysical, then the proposition that minds are nonphysical will be true, and hence will be one of the propositions in the true account of the world.

There is no requirement that one be an absolutist about everything. One might simply be a local absolutist, believing, for instance, that there is one true account of the physical facts, while leaving it open whether there may be a plurality of facts about, e.g., morality. Indeed, such intermediate positions are quite popular. But when one reads the fine print of such views, it usually turns out that the facts about what ultimately exists—the "real facts," in other words—are absolute, and the "facts" that admit of a plurality are relegated to second-class citizenship. Mixed positions generally give priority to those facts considered absolute. For this reason, throughout the book I will concentrate on *metaphysical* absolutism and pluralism, on facts about ultimate or basic reality. In my general description of both views, however, I shall be sketching absolutism and pluralism as they would apply to any fact or proposition.

1.3   The Move to Pluralism

Metaphysical pluralism is often seen as a consequence of a particular theory of truth. For example, advocates of epistemic theories of truth, such as the coherence and pragmatist theories, often take their views to entail some sort of pluralism. If the truth of a proposition consisted in its pragmatic consequences, then seemingly conflicting views could both be true if they happened to have the same practical consequences for our everyday lives. But since the goal of this book is to show how a robust pluralism is consistent with a *non*epistemic theory of truth, I shall not be concentrating on epistemic theories of truth as ways of motivating a pluralist perspective.

Once we put issues relating to truth on one side, the most common motivation for metaphysical pluralism is the peculiar intractability of metaphysical debate. As I noted above, this sort of intuition pump is familiar to us from debates over morality or aesthetics. I am not interested in convincing anyone that any particular metaphysical debate is perverse. Rather, I want only to explain how these sorts of debates can provide motivation for metaphysical pluralism. Whether that motivation is or should be compelling for everyone is a different issue, although I suspect it isn't and never will be (the existence of disagreement on these matters is part of the point, after all). In any event, examples are not difficult to find, since questions about the ultimate nature of the world are as numerous as its contents.

Consider problems of personal identity, for instance.[11] It is possible to split the hemispheres of the human brain without killing the patient. We also know that people can survive with just one half of their brain intact. Suppose that we could split your brain and, while keeping the hemispheres intact and operational, transplant each half into another body. Let us imagine (plausibly) that each of the resulting people has your character as well as apparent memories of your life. How many people are there now, and what has happened to you? One theory might maintain that you have died, to be replaced by two new people (but if people can survive with half of their brain intact, why can't you survive with both halves intact?). Another theory might claim that you survive as one of the people (but which one?). Yet another theory might claim that you survive as both (but how could one person be two people?). A fourth theory maintains that in fact, prior to the operation, your body housed two "coincident" people that have only now separated. The theories agree on all the facts about the operation and other perceived events but disagree about how many people have survived the operation.

As an example of Hilary Putnam's illustrates, ontologies have consequences for even the most mundane questions.[12] Imagine that I ask a friend how many objects are in my study. After counting the books, computer, desk, chair, and whatnot, she announces that there are exactly one hundred objects in the room. One sort of philosopher might claim that even though my friend's answer is acceptable loosely speaking, *strictly* speaking she is incorrect because she has forgotten to count the molecules and atoms in the room. Or consider the mereologist, who believes that every part of an object is itself an object, and that for every pair of objects, there is an object that has each member of that pair as parts. He will insist that we also count the "mereological sums" of the various macro and micro objects in the room, such as the object made up of the sum of the tip of my nose and my keyboard. If either of these philosophers is right, it would seem that the number of objects in the room is much larger than what my friend believes.

Another (and historically more important) example is the debate over substance. Roughly speaking, a substance is basic or fundamental in that it *has* properties but is itself not a property of something else. According to a philosopher like Aristotle, many substances and types of substances exist, all of which endure through time, have identity conditions, possess properties both accidentally and essentially, etc. A particular person, on the Aristotelian view, is just one of these substances. But to a monist like Spinoza, persons are not basic enough to be substances. According to Spinoza, there is ultimately only *one* substance—the universe as a whole. He calls this one substance both "God" and "Nature." Of course, it may *appear* to us that trees and humans are different substances, but ultimately, trees, persons, and mountains are just different modes or properties of the one *underlying* substance. Individual persons exist, of course, but they are "substances" only loosely speaking; strictly speaking, there is only the one substance, and a person such as yourself is simply a mode of that substance, a way in which it is at a particular time.

For a fourth type of example, we can turn to mathematics and logic. Consider numbers. Are they to be identified with the all too perishable scratches we make on a blackboard or the ideas we have when making those marks or something altogether different, as Plato thought, existing outside of space and time? Surely, it seems, they must be *something*. Or take points on a Euclidean plane. Points can be taken to be basic abstract particulars, sets of convergent spheres, composed of intersecting lines, or logical constructions out of volumes.[13] Every one of these answers would seem to be in conflict with the others: to say that points are particulars, for instance, is meant to rule out that they are "really" intersecting lines. Similar debates can take place over the ontological status of sets, functions, propositions, possible worlds, and properties. We can even ask these questions about a piece of music, such as Beethoven's Fifth Symphony. The symphony exists, of course, but what is it? Is it a repeatable pattern of sound made by instruments (and if so, *where* is this pattern?) or the actual sounds themselves (meaning that Beethoven's symphony doesn't exist when no one is playing it)? Or is the answer something else altogether?

The perplexity that we feel when faced with this and similar examples arises because, on the one hand, the competing answers seem straightforwardly incompatible: they appear to describe the world in radically different ways. For surely (we might think) there are exactly one hundred items in the room or there are exactly some other number of items. But on the other hand, the theories are also frustratingly equivalent in a certain sense. They are equivalent in that which theory we employ will make no difference to our predictions, (nonmetaphysical) explanations, and scientific practices in general.[14] As far as our everyday lives are concerned (and here I include our scientific lives), it is simply irrelevant whether there are "really" mereological sums in my study or whether propositions are sets of possible worlds or possible worlds sets of propositions. Of course, it *would* be news if a philosopher could convince us, with arguments to the effect that they don't exist, to stop even *appearing* to refer to, e.g., numbers or physical objects or other items we normally appeal to in our everyday lives. But most philosophers who deny the existence of such objects do *not* believe that their theories force a cultural change. Rather, like Berkeley, they are prone to argue that their radical ontological views either capture, or are consistent with, our ordinary beliefs. The contemporary ontologist can even employ various semantic techniques that allow him to maintain his thesis without revising the truth values of our ordinary talk about tables, chairs, and whatnot. One contemporary ontologist, for instance, maintains that he can consistently deny that there are any tables, chairs, and "middle-sized dry-goods" in general without thereby contradicting anything that the ordinary person believes or says.[15]

So the intuition that these debates are incapable of being absolutely resolved is not simply due to the fact that there is wide disagreement. Rather, it is the *nature of the disagreement* that fosters the relativist intuition: the metaphysical concepts themselves seem to be responsible for the suspicion that there is no absolute way to resolve the dispute.

I stress that you can have pluralist intuitions without having any allegiance to verificationism. According to classical verificationism, propositions that cannot be empirically verified are meaningless. What the typical verificationist and the pluralist share in common is the belief that metaphysical debates are unsolvable in any absolute sense. But that is where the similarity stops. Unlike the verificationist, the pluralist does not conclude that metaphysical propositions are meaningless because they cannot be verified. Rather, pluralism is the view that there can be more than one true answer to these questions—not that every answer is meaningless.

1.4   Metaphysical Pluralism

Like its opposite, metaphysical pluralism has two sides: one representational (concerning content), the other concerning fact. These views are usefully characterized as *relativist*, but the reader is urged not to place undue weight on this term. "Relativism," besides having become a dirty word in some circles, can be highly misleading, since wildly different views often bear the title. Most important, I stress that the following principles are slogans. They are the initial characterizations of a pluralist view whose heart is far more complex than concentration on them alone would make it seem. Nonetheless, slogans have their place, in philosophy as well as in politics. Here they are useful because they allow me to speak generally about the most important consequences of pluralism.

A central point of the last section was that pluralism can be motivated by the perplexing nature of certain metaphysical debates. What does it mean to say that there are more than ten objects in the room, or that the world contains many substances, or that numbers and symphonies exist? It is tempting to hold that the metaphysical content of these assertions is simply indeterminate absent any appeal to a wider context. This is precisely the intuition behind *content relativism* with regard to metaphysics. Just as there appears to be no objective way of settling the disputes discussed in the last section, so there is no external fact, independent of my conceptual scheme, that determines the truth conditions for my claim about, e.g., the number of objects. The proposition that I am expressing, what I am saying about the nature of reality, can be understood only by appealing to a scheme. As Hilary Putnam has claimed, "It is characteristic of [my] view to hold that *What objects does the world consist of?* is a question which only makes sense to ask *within* a theory or description" (Putnam 1981, 49). That this question makes sense *only within* a conceptual scheme implies that any answer to it must be relative, in some way or other, to a way of dividing up the world. And since there can be more than one way to do that, there can be more than one true answer to our questions about ultimate reality.

On my understanding, the underlying position here is that the content of an assertion is intrinsically related to a conceptual scheme. (We will see later that conceptual schemes are themselves parts of an organic whole that I call a "worldview," but such details are better left off for the moment.) Again, one can distinguish propositions by their truth conditions; so another way of putting the point would be to say that truth conditions are determinate only within a conceptual scheme. There are no determinate propositions independent of schemes; content is internal. In effect, propositions, true or false, are implicitly *indexed* to some conceptual scheme or schemes. This intrinsic connection between scheme and content means that the proposition that there is more than one object is, in a sense, underdescribed. It should be understood as the proposition that there is more than one object relative to C. I don't mean to imply that the ordinary person knows that the contents of her beliefs are relative or that she intends to express propositions that are.[16] Content relativism is a theory about the propositions we express, not about our intentions. In sum, content relativism about some domain is the view that if one were to give a complete and comprehensive analysis of a proposition in that domain, one would have to refer in that analysis to the conceptual scheme in which that proposition is expressed.

It may be helpful to quickly compare the debate over content relativism and content absolutism with a somewhat analogous debate between spatial relativism and spatial absolutism. The spatial relativist holds that all the facts about motion and location are facts about how objects are spatially related. Thus a proposition about the motion of some object is true or false only relative to a material frame of reference. The spatial absolutist, on the other hand, believes that there are also absolute facts about motion. The absolute facts about motion and location concern how objects are moving and located relative to absolute space. According to the spatial relativist, there is no proposition expressed by the sentence "The truck is moving" considered independently of any frame of reference. As uttered by someone on the sidewalk, for instance, the proposition that sentence will express could be the proposition that the truck is moving relative to the sidewalk. The metaphysical pluralist makes a similar claim:

there are no propositions independent of conceptual frameworks. So we can think of the pluralist's notion of content relativity as being in some ways an analogous extension of the spatial relativist's belief in the relativity of all propositions about motion. The spatial relativist claims that the content of the statement "The truck is moving" is relative to a particular material frame of reference; the metaphysical pluralist holds that the proposition that there is only one substance is relative to a conceptual scheme. Both claim that content is relative.

Yet we shouldn't overdo the analogy. The relativism of the spatial relativist is far more limited than the relativism involved in metaphysical pluralism. Metaphysical pluralism is a relativism about ultimate ontology, and as such it arguably entails a much more global pluralism. As we shall see throughout this book, the dramatically wider scope of metaphysical pluralism raises numerous problems—problems about self-reference, for instance—that spatial relativism does not.[17]

The second face of metaphysical pluralism is embraced by Hilary Putnam when he says, "To talk of 'facts' without specifying the language to be used is to talk of nothing" (1989, 114). Facts are *internal* to conceptual schemes, or ways of dividing the world into objects, among which there can be equally acceptable alternatives. Indeed, for the pluralist, every state of affairs, whether it obtains or not in the actual world, is internally related or relative to some conceptual scheme. Yet since facts concern us more than nonfacts (or states of affairs that don't obtain), I shall for the most part ignore the distinction and simply call the second face of pluralism *fact relativism*. The view can be stated in several different ways; since I am assuming an ontologically innocent sense of "fact," there is no reason to state "fact relativism" in terms of facts. I can make the same point by saying that every obtaining state of affairs obtains only within a scheme, or that objects exist and have properties only relative to schemes. As Putnam infamously declares, "Objects do not exist independently of conceptual schemes. We cut up the world into objects when we introduce one or another form of description" (1981, 52). Once this relativity is acknowledged, the pluralist's view that there can be irreducibly different but equally true perspectives on reality begins to take on more shape. For now we can say (from within a certain scheme, of course) that relative to an Aristotelian scheme, there is more than one substance, but relative to a Spinozistic scheme, there is only one. Or, from one standpoint there are one hundered objects in my study, while from another (the mereologist's) there are millions more.

One might think that what the pluralist is advocating here is simply a radical extension of something everyone recognizes in other circumstances. All of us believe that you and I aren't really disagreeing if you, using one system of measurement, report the temperature to be 0 and I, using a different system of measurement, report it to be 32. If we don't realize that we are using different systems, we might think we disagree. But once we realize that we are using different schemes of measurement, we can see that we are actually reporting on the same thermal state of affairs. It is tempting to say that the pluralist's point, then, is that ontological disputes are analogous to the "thermal dispute" just described. Yet again, the analogy is only so helpful. In the example, we take it for granted that there is a neutral standpoint, an absolute point of reference by which we can judge the situation. For the metaphysical pluralist, there is no such point of reference; *every* reporting of an ontological fact is done within a conceptual scheme or metaphysical perspective. There is no scheme-neutral way of making a report about the world. It would be a mistake to search for the scheme that tells it like it "really" is—there is no such thing.

My laying out these issues clearly owes much to the work of Hilary Putnam, the most prominent of contemporary pluralists. Yet it is important not to overstate the similarities between the views discussed here and the positions Putnam labels "metaphysical realism" and "internal realism." According to Putnam, metaphysical realism is comprised of three views:

The world consists of some fixed totality of mind-independent objects. There is exactly one and only one true description of "the way the world is." Truth involves some sort of correspondence relation between words and thought-signs and external things and sets of things. (1981, 49)

The first of the three criteria suggests that a main difference between metaphysical realism and Putnam's internal realism concerns the existence of mind-independent objects. As we shall see in chapter 4, there are senses of "mind-independent" according to which this difference is also present in the pluralism/absolutism debate, but there are other, perhaps more important, senses in which it is not. What I've been calling content absolutism is essentially the second component of Putnam's metaphysical realism: there is exactly one and only one true account of the world. Putnam's third component of metaphysical realism, however, is not part of my description of absolutism. The thesis that absolutism is logically distinct from the "correspondence theory of truth" is essentially the flipside of the main thesis of this book, namely that pluralism is consistent with realism with regard to truth.

1.5 Facts and Content

Just as the two faces of absolutism are connected, the two sides of pluralism, fact and content relativism, are best seen as two aspects of one view. Indeed, there is a strong case to be made for thinking that, given a few innocuous premises, each aspect of pluralism logically entails the other. Strictly speaking, their logical connection is not needed for the main claim of the book, namely that metaphysical pluralism is consistent with realism about truth. To accept *this* claim, and the arguments I shall marshal. on its behalf, one need only accept that pluralism is committed to a relativity of *both* fact and content. Nonetheless, the argument for their connection is of more than technical interest. It demonstrates the depth to which the pluralist believes that the world and content are interwoven, and furthermore, it suggests a helpful strategy for presenting the details of pluralism itself.

The less controversial direction of the connection goes from fact relativism to content relativism. Suppose fact relativism is true: there are no facts independent of conceptual schemes. The fact that grass is green is relative to C. If so, then the proposition that grass is green must also be relative to C. The connecting premise is again the T-schema, or the truism that the content of a statement determines the necessary and sufficient conditions under which it is true. If facts are relative, it follows that when I state the fact that grass is green in C, what I am saying, the proposition I am expressing, is that grass is green in C. Intuitively, if facts are relative, then whatever truths I express must also be relative as well. Content relativism follows naturally from fact relativism.[18]

The more controversial point is that content relativism also leads to fact relativism. Many philosophers are inclined to accept the former but deny the latter. After all, one might say, it is one thing to acknowledge that our *representations* of the world intrinsically depend on conceptual schemes, but another matter entirely to believe that this requires that the world itself be relative in some way. Even if our thoughts about objects are relative to conceptual schemes, this doesn't entail that "objects do not exist independently of our conceptual scheme" (Putnam 1981, 52). Or as Paul Moser has recently claimed,

> Saying and asking are, naturally enough, "relative to some background language," but it does not follow that the objects about which one says or asks something are similarly relative. . . . Linguistic relativity of the notions and statements of an ontology does not entail linguistic relativity of what those notions and statements are about. (1993, 37)

Similar claims, most of which are directed against Hilary Putnam's "internal realism," run throughout the literature.[19] Our judgments, propositions, and concepts may be relative, the story goes, but the world is not.[20]

The argument for the contrary opinion is straightforward. Assume content relativism with regard to the proposition that grass is green. We can summarize this by saying that the proposition that grass is green is the proposition that grass is green relative to C. Now assume, harmlessly, that this proposition is true. If so, then the following instance of the T-schema must be true a priori:

The proposition that grass is green relative to C is true if, and only if, grass is green relative to C.

The content of my statement, in other words, necessarily determines the conditions under which it is true. And the conditions under which it is true that grass is green relative to C are when grass is green relative to C. If so, then the relevant instance of the F-schema is also true a priori:

Grass is green relative to C if, and only if, it is a fact that grass is green relative to C.

It follows from the transitivity of the biconditional that

The proposition that grass is green relative to C is true if, and only if, it is a fact that grass is green relative to C.

From this, of course, we can deduce that it is a fact that grass is green relative to C. The existence of a true relative proposition entails a relative fact.

I'll call the above argument the *T-argument*. The T-argument is persuasive in part because it is so simple. To show a connection between the two faces of pluralism or absolutism, we need only rely on three additional premises: the truth of some of what we say, and instances of the T and F schemata. And as I noted earlier, instances of the T and F schemata are as plausible candidates for necessary truths as any statements one might imagine. These principles mark out our concepts of truth and fact; hence instances of the T and F schemata are *intensional*, as opposed to extensional, truths. This distinguishes the T-schema from Tarski's Convention T, or what is sometimes called the "disquotational schema." The main difference is that instances of what I am calling the T-schema are necessary, a priori, truths. It *couldn't* be true that grass is green unless grass *is* green and vice versa, and it can't be a fact that grass is green unless grass is really green and conversely.[21]

No particular theory of truth or fact needs to be assumed in order for the T-argument to go through. To demonstrate the argument's neutrality with regard to truth, propositions, and facts alike, let's suppose (for demonstration purposes only) that, following Davidson (1967) and Field (1972), the concept of truth for natural languages can be understood through a Tarskian recursive definition. On this view, it is interpreted sentence tokens that are true. Roughly speaking, sentences of the form "x is F" are true in virtue of the fact that there exists an object that "x" designates and that is among the objects to which "F" applies. On this theory, the content or meaning of a sentence in a language is determined by its extensional interpretation, while talk about facts is understood as talk about objects having particular properties (or being members of certain classes). Truth is the relationship (the correspondence) between the component parts of an interpreted sentence and certain objects and properties in the world. Under this line of thought, then, fact relativism amounts to saying that objects have the properties they do only relative to a conceptual scheme.[22] Similarly, content relativism is the view that sentential *interpretations* are relative to conceptual schemes. This isn't simply to repeat the point that the content or meaning of a sentence depends on its interpretation within a language. On that both the pluralist and the absolutist can agree. Rather, it means that there are no scheme-independent facts that determine interpretations. As Putnam sometimes puts it, the world does not interpret sentences for us; independent of conceptual schemes there is literally no fact of the matter about the references of our terms. (1987, 32–33). Now suppose that we understand the sentence token "Grass is green" under an interpretation that takes it to mean that grass is green. The content relativist will hold this interpretation to be relative to a particular conceptual scheme. If so, then the sentence "Grass is green" (under the *C*-relative interpretation) will be true just when "grass" refers to grass *relative to C*, and "green" to greenness *relative to C*, and grass actually is green *relative to C*. Think of it this way. The content, or meaning, of a sentence token or utterance specifies the conditions under which that token is true. When the content is relative, the truth conditions must be relative. If the claim in question is "*x* exists" and its content is "*x* exists relative to *C*," then the conditions for its truth are that *x* exists relative to *C*. The statement is true when that scheme-relative state of affairs obtains, and false otherwise. For the pluralist, this means that it is possible that *x* exists relative to *C* but *not* relative to *D* and, furthermore, that there is no scheme-independent fact of the matter about who is right. Once we assume content relativism and take it that some of what we say is true, we must embrace fact relativism as well. As Putnam says, "To talk of 'facts' without specifying the language to be used is to talk of nothing" (Putnam 1989, 114).

The T-argument provides a strong case for thinking that fact and content relativism plausibly stand or fall together. At the very least, it provides a significant challenge to those who would accept the relativity of representations while denying the relativity of what is represented. Furthermore, the logical connection between the two faces of pluralism suggests a way of tackling the details of the pluralist view. If we can explain pluralism's relativistic view of propositional content, an understanding of fact relativism will follow in train. In effect, this will be my strategy for the next two chapters.

1.6   Three Objections

If pluralism were obviously incoherent, then an argument for its consistency with anything would be of little value. So I will spend some time examining the arguments that imply that the view is hopelessly confused (or not even a distinct philosophical view at all). As it turns out, I believe these to be the most powerful objections to pluralism anyway. And lest the reader think I am blissfully ignorant of the difficulty of my task, I think it best to describe these problems at the start.

As a whole, this essay could be taken as a refutation of what is perhaps the most popular objection to pluralism. That objection is that metaphysical pluralism implies an incoherent epistemic or relativist concept of truth. Since I think that pluralism is consistent with realism about the concept of truth, I obviously disagree. But as I noted in the first section, even most pluralists take their view to imply an antirealist theory of truth. Putnam, for instance, has denied that pluralism entails a relativist account of truth but he has argued that pluralism does imply an epistemic account of the concept, that is, one which defines truth in terms of justification:

> If objects are, at least when you get small enough, or large enough, or theoretical enough, theory-dependent, then the whole idea of truth being defined or explained in terms of "correspondence" between items in a language and items in a fixed theory-independent reality has to be given up. The picture I propose instead is . . . that truth comes to no more than idealized rational acceptability. (Putman 1990, 41)

There are reasons to think that Putnam has now abandoned an overtly epistemic theory of truth (1994b). Nonetheless, claims such as the above have been common in most of Putnam's work since 1980.[23] Further, Putnam's view that his pluralist metaphysics commits him to an epistemic account of truth is, as far as I know, not questioned by his critics.[24] And if one believes that such a view is incoherent, then obviously pluralism is incoherent as well.

A second common criticism of metaphysical pluralism alleges that the view is really just a disguised form of idealism—the doctrine that everything is either mental or dependent on minds in some way. The reasoning behind this suspicion is easy to see. I have said that fact relativism involves the relativity of facts to conceptual schemes, and I have noted that this thesis can be expressed in terms of objects and their properties being relative to schemes. Thus, according to pluralism what exists does so only relative to conceptual schemes. So it seems that the pluralist must acknowledge that without conceptual schemes, the world would cease to exist.

A third objection is even more troubling, and will accordingly be more difficult to solve. Rather than concentrating on the alleged implications of metaphysical pluralism, it raises the possibility that no such position is in fact possible. I'll call this objection the *consistency dilemma*. Like pluralism itself, the consistency dilemma has two aspects: one aimed at content or representation, the other involving facts and the world.

The pluralist alleges that there can be more than one true account of the world. Now consider two such metaphysical perspectives, *A* and *B* that meet whatever criteria the pluralist requires for perspectives to be "equally" true. Either these perspectives are consistent with each other, or they are not. If not, then by virtue of her statement that *A* and *B* are equally true, the pluralist is in danger of being committed to the truth of contradictions. Now as we've seen, the metaphysical pluralist avoids this latter problem by relativization. On her view, facts and content are relative: *A* can be the case relative to C_1, and $\sim A$ relative to C_2 without contradiction. But the point of the present objection is that this move fails to get the pluralist off the hook. The real problem for pluralism is not the *inconsistency* but the *consistency of schemes*. In other words, given the consistency between *A* and *B* that the relativization of fact apparently implies, the pluralist must explain how it is legitimate to talk about *incompatible* but equally true schemes in the first place. Specifically, if *A* and *B* are consistent, then either (1) *A* and *B* are expressing the same absolute truths in different languages (they are "notational variants") or (2) *A* and *B* are simply concerned with different subject matters altogether. But even the most hard-headed absolutist could grant either possibility, for both (1) and (2) are consistent with absolutism! The upshot of the consistency dilemma is that metaphysical pluralism does not succeed in presenting a distinct philosophical position.

The ontological face of the consistency dilemma could just as well be called the *many-worlds problem*. It arises in exactly the same way. Following Wittgenstein, we could say that the world is everything that is the case. That is, the world is the sum of all the facts. Now according to the pluralist, all facts are relative to conceptual schemes. Hence the pluralist is committed either to the existence of many worlds of facts—one world for each conceptual scheme—or to the existence of one world of facts that all conceptual perspectives are perspectives of. If the former is the case, if there is one world for each conceptual scheme, then not only has the pluralist adopted a bizarre ontology on which worlds are like bubbles insulated from each other by the fragile barriers of concepts, she has apparently committed herself to absolutism. On such a picture, there will be one true story (an absolutely true account) of each individual world. (And the conjunction of those stories will be an absolute account of every world.) On the other hand, if the pluralist holds that there is only one world that all schemes represent, then presumably there will also be one true account of that world. And again, pluralism disappears as a distinct philosophical view.

These objections are not the only criticisms one might raise against pluralism, but they are the most prominent and compelling. As I noted, the objection from truth will be answered by the core thesis of this book. But the idealism objection, consistency dilemma, and its ontological face, the many-worlds problem, are no less important. If metaphysical pluralism cannot effectively answer these objections, then the conjunction of realism about truth and pluralism (what I called in the introduction relativistic Kantianism) becomes a less interesting philosophical position.

The next step, therefore, is to delve deeper into the details of pluralism, particularly into the notion of content relativism. Only after I have laid out these details will the answers to the objections above become clear. I'll begin by examining what propositions and facts are relative to: conceptual schemes.

2

Understanding Conceptual Schemes

Metaphysics is the attempt to find out what absolute presuppositions have been made by this or that person or group of persons, on this or that occasion or group of occasions, in the course of this or that piece of thinking.

R. G. Collingwood

2.1 Three Models

The idea that human beings can have different perspectives, engage in distinct forms of life, or use different conceptual schemes is an essential element of any pluralism. Yet despite pervasive use of such notions in the philosophical literature, little is ever said about the nature of conceptual schemes beyond noting that they are "a way of organizing the world" or "a way of categorizing the world into objects."[1] These remarks paint some sort of picture but leave quite a bit to the imagination. What are these "ways" of seeing the world, exactly? To paraphrase James, one wants the *particular go of it*.[2] But any attempt by the pluralist to fill in the picture, to give the particulars, risks running afoul of objections like Donald Davidson's influential critique of the notion. According to Davidson (1984), the very idea of a plurality of conceptual schemes—and hence the concept of a scheme itself—is bankrupt and incoherent. The key is to find a notion of conceptual schemes that can avoid these criticisms even while it helps us round out our understanding of metaphysical pluralism.

Rooting around in the historical underbrush for the sources of our ideas about conceptual schemes, one finds two dominant models lurking beneath writings related to the topic. These models stem from Kant and Quine, even though neither is *explicit* in the work of either philosopher.

Quine, for instance, has said that he used the term "as ordinary language, serving no technical function," and Kant certainly can't be said to have had a view of conceptual schemes properly so called.[3] Yet their respective ideas about concepts and the world do mark out two ends of a spectrum. They provide clear starting points from which we can build two different ways of looking at conceptual schemes. In turn, the problems of each reveal a middle path between them—a third way of understanding conceptual schemes that helps us to fill in the details of the pluralist picture in a new and more powerful way.

2.2   The Kantian Model

If one had to name a single origin of the idea of a conceptual framework, it would probably be Kant's view that all possible experience has a structure or *form*. That structure, according to Kant, is due to the joint work of two faculties of the mind, the "sensibility" and the "understanding." The sensibility subsumes all of our sensory experience under the pure forms of intuition, space, and time, while the understanding applies what Kant called "pure" concepts, or the categories, each of which must have some application in experience if we are to have any experience at all. Thus, the fact that we experience the world of "outer sense"—the world beyond our skins—as spatial, temporal, and causally ordered is due to the faculties of our mind—to their application of the concepts of space, time, and causality. These concepts organize raw preexperiential sensory intuition into experience of a world with sizes and shapes, befores and afters, causes and effects. No doubt, you and I will apply many different *specific* concepts (concepts like dog or cat) to experience. But certain fundamental concepts shape the experience of all thinkers: the concepts of space and time (the forms of intuition) and the pure concepts of the understanding (the categories). For Kant, these concepts are necessarily the form for *all* possible experience; without the application of such concepts, there is no experience at all.

The Kantian model (KM) of a conceptual scheme, therefore, is that of a scheme of concepts with which any thinker informs or structures experience.[4] From this brief introduction, I think we can extrapolate a good picture of the model. My strategy for doing so will center around the following questions:

1. What are the primary components of the scheme?
2. What are the criteria of identity for schemes?
3. Does the model require the analytic/synthetic or related distinctions?
4. What is the structural nature of a scheme?

Let us see how the advocate of the Kantian Model would answer these questions.

KM1   *The primary components of a conceptual scheme are mental.*

Roughly speaking, Kant's transcendental psychology took concepts to be creatures of the mind; they were capacities the mind had to organize raw unconceptualized intuitions into conscious experience. Doubtless, Kant believed that we could and would reflect our concepts in language, but for Kant, the categorical concepts, at least, are—to speak loosely—"hardwired" into the nature of the mind itself.[5] So, according to KM, conceptual schemes are obviously just that: schemes of concepts, where a concept is a mental entity, a way of thinking about something, that is typically expressed linguistically as a general term.

KM2   *The criteria of identity for schemes lies with their categorical and formal concepts.*

Kant believed that if one wanted to understand knowledge and conceptualization, one needed to understand the nature and extent of the categories and the pure forms of intuition. The pure concepts of the understanding and the forms of intuition together limit and structure our knowledge. If we take "categorical and formal concepts" to stand for both the pure concepts and the forms of intuition, this suggests a natural criterion of identity for conceptual schemes on KM: conceptual schemes are identical if, and only if, they share the same categorical and formal concepts.[6]

KM3   *Conceptual schemes involve a commitment to the analytic/synthetic distinction.*

According to KM, conceptual schemes are fixed frameworks of categorical concepts used to cognize any possible or actual experience. This picture entails a difference between the concepts that *form the scheme* and *what* it is that the scheme is structuring or organizing—what it is a scheme of, in other words. This in turn forces a difference, on the linguistic front, between sentences true in virtue of their concepts ("All bachelors are unmarried") and sentences true in virtue of their content, or how things stand in the world ("There are more than ten words on this page"). The former express analytic statements—statements where the concept of the predicate is included within the concept of the subject, as Kant would say—while the latter type of sentences express synthetic statements. In short, KM separates statements that describe the scheme of concepts itself and statements that describe the world.

KM4   *Schemes have a foundationalist structure.*

This proposition, in essence, is already implied by the first three views above. According to the picture those views sketch for us, a conceptual scheme is an *organized* network of concepts: "organized" because some nodes of the network, some concepts, are more central to the network than others. This structure is analogous to foundationalist views of the structure of epistemic justification, according to which our knowledge is founded on basic beliefs that are themselves not justified by other beliefs. Our present concern is with conceptual, not epistemic, architecture, but there remains a structural analogy. According to KM, foundational concepts are those basic and general concepts such as Kant's categorical concepts. These concepts are foundational in that KM implies that all concept application presupposes the existence and application of categorical/formal concepts. For all possible experience necessarily presupposes a certain *fixed* set of these concepts, and hence, since experience is obviously necessary to form more specific, noncategorical concepts, the fixed set of foundational concepts are indirectly necessary for the formation and application of any concepts, at any time, for any thinker. Categorical and formal concepts are the bedrock of the Kantian model of a conceptual scheme.

I hope that the reader familiar with the philosophical literature will find this set of ideas familiar, whether or not, in the reader's opinion, they accurately represent Kant's own views. For KM1 through KM4 are surely *Kantian* views; that is, they represent ideas traditionally attributed to Kant. I also believe that these ideas helped set the stage for all later philosophizing about mind and world and formed the backdrop against which other philosophers reacted. Accordingly, I'll refrain from boring the reader with a catalogue of KM's influence in the literature. Nor will I try to demonstrate the myriad faults and shortcomings of KM, not only because such a discussion would be too long for present purposes but also because it would also be somewhat pointless, since I suspect that most readers will not be drawn to KM in the first place. It is, after all, the Quinean model (QM) that is the most pervasive view of conceptual schemes today, and more or less, its virtues are that it lacks the vices of its Kantian cousin. What one *can* say is that KM is essentially useless for our project of understanding metaphysical pluralism. KM does not allow for the possibility of a pluralism about schemes, since the categories are to act as the form for all possible experience. Nor does its embrace of foundationalism and a hard difference between the analytic and synthetic seem friendly to the general drift of the relativist's view. Yet as we shall see, QM has severe shortcomings in this area all its own.

2.3   The Quinean Model

With the advent in philosophy of the so-called "linguistic turn," the broadly Kantian model of conceptual schemes was gradually abandoned even as the notion of a conceptual scheme itself became more familiar. Just one of many reasons for this change was the popularity of the idea that thought is intrinsically connected with, perhaps even identical to, language. The fact that languages are public—the fact that they can be dissected and discussed in the open air and are therefore much more palatable to the scientific mind than murky Kantian "categories"—understandably led to a concentration on terms and sentences over concepts. By the 1950s we find Rudolph Carnap talking naturally and reflexively about *linguistic frameworks* or languages, in much the same way an earlier philosopher (or a later one) might discuss conceptual frameworks.[7] Together with this identification of schemes with languages came a corresponding shift from concepts—or subsentential components—to sentences as the elements of the scheme. For it is sentences that are the prime bearers of linguistic meaning. The result was a view that took conceptual schemes as frameworks of sentences instead of concepts. In effect, there was a shift from one picture to another. Quine:

The totality of our so-called knowledge or beliefs, from the most casual matters of geography and history to the profoundest laws of atomic physics or even mathematics and logic, is a man-made fabric which impinges on experience at the edges. (1953, 42)

Quine is advocating his view that our conceptual scheme is a tapestry, fabric, or web, no parts of which are immune from revision or alteration, and hence no parts of which are essentially more basic than others. Our conceptual scheme, according to this view, is not a framework of "concepts" but simply that set of (revisable) sentences that we accept in light of experience. Again, we can boil down the picture of conceptual schemes suggested by Quine's writings into four claims.

QM1   *Conceptual schemes are "languages"; they are composed of sentences accepted as true.*

Put in an intentional mode, a scheme, according to QM, is the "totality of our so-called knowledge or beliefs" ("so-called" because some of the beliefs that fit experience now we may later revise or drop entirely); more accurately, the fabric spoken of above "is a fabric of sentences accepted in science as true, however provisionally" (1981, 40). And hence where Quine has spoken of a conceptual scheme, he says, "I could have spoken of a language" (1981, 41).

QM2   *The criteria for identity is intertranslatability.*

This is a result of QM's identification of schemes with languages. As Quine himself noted, once I've "correlated" your sentences with mine, I've established that you share the same scheme, for "what further criterion for sameness of conceptual scheme can be imagined?" (1969, 5). Alternative schemes are simply those languages not intertranslatable with ours, and identical conceptual schemes those that are. In a true Quinean spirit, one can make this more precise by taking the notion of translation here to be purely extensional and define a conceptual scheme as follows. Take some language L that consists of (a possibly indefinite) number of declarative sentences and is free from vagueness and ambiguity. An "interpretation" of L will assign extensions to each general term of L and designata to each of its singular terms. Worries about indeterminacy aside, a translation of sentence S from L into sentence S^* of L^* will be successful if, and only if, S and S^* have the same extension and designata assigned to their respective terms. Thus we can say that L and L^* share the same conceptual scheme just when both admit of the very same extensional interpretation. In short, schemes are functions from languages to extensional "interpretations."

QM3   *The notion of a conceptual scheme does not entail the analytic/ synthetic distinction.*

The final blow to the Kantian understanding of a conceptual scheme came with the popular rejection of the analytic/synthetic and related distinctions. In Quine's view, giving up on the analytic/synthetic distinction is giving up on the idea that some statements hold in light of experience and others hold come what may. Rather, any statement is revisable; there is no division between statements true in virtue of concepts and statements true in virtue of experience. According to Quine, one should instead look at one's conceptual scheme as a interconnected "web of belief." In the center of the web are those beliefs we are most reluctant to give up; on the fringes, beliefs we would more readily revise in the light of experience. But no belief or statement, not even "All bachelors are unmarried" is "conceptually or analytically" true. There are no statements true in virtue of their concepts alone—true by definition. As a consequence, the "fixed framework of concepts" model is replaced by a view in which "meaning is contaminated by theory." The net result is that instead of thinking of our conceptual scheme as being composed of two elements, concepts or meanings on the one hand and beliefs about the world on the other, we should think of it as a whole language standing in relation to the world or experience as a whole.

QM4   *The structure of schemes is "coherentist" in nature.*

With the advent of these views, a "holistic" notion of a conceptual scheme was born. Rather than a fixed foundation of concepts and a house of *in*formed content, we have a web of belief that confronts reality as a corporate body. We have the Quinean model of conceptual schemes.

Once again, I expect that I needn't belabor the influence of QM1 through QM4 on philosophical thought. They encapsulate a point of view about schemes whose roots spread throughout our intellectual land-scape. But it is worth explicitly noting two important fallouts of QM, which, if not entailed by QM directly, certainly seem to many to be natural consequences of the Quinean model. First, there is the possibility of plural schemes. QM allows for a shift away from the absolutism of KM—according to which there is one and only one scheme possible—toward a more pluralistic view. According to QM, schemes are languages, and on the face of it at least, there can surely be more than one language, and hence more than one conceptual scheme. Second, there is the so-called "incommensurability" thesis. Following the lead of Quine's rejection of the analytic/synthetic distinction, Thomas Kuhn (1962) famously argued that the progress of science not only alters what we believe, it alters the concepts that we use to express those beliefs. Since meanings change as theories change, one can no longer distinguish between sentences of the theory (scheme, language) that describe what the theory is about and sentences that define the meanings of the terms or the concepts of the theory. The meaning of terms such as "force," "space," and "motion" should be seen not as invariant but as dependent on and responsive to changes in scientific data and method. For instance, Einstein's theories of relativity, according to Kuhn, can no longer be regarded as simply giving us new insight into the nature of space and time—insight that Newton's theory lacked—but must be viewed as developing entirely new concepts of space and time. Newton and Einstein are to be seen not as offering contrary theories on the nature of one thing, e.g., space, but as discussing entirely different things while using the same word. In Kuhn's language, their respective conceptual schemes are "incommensurable." For both of these reasons, the tolerance of pluralism and the implication that different schemes are incommensurable, QM seems more compatible with metaphysical pluralism.

QM is the target of Davidson's famous paper "On the Very Idea of a Conceptual Scheme" (1984). Davidson explicitly identifies schemes with languages and points out that contemporary proponents of the idea of a conceptual scheme have abandoned the analytic/synthetic doctrine. His most basic criticism of the notion takes the form of a dilemma. If schemes are languages, then (according to QM2) schemes will be distinct only if we cannot translate between them. For if we could translate between the languages, then we would have not two distinct ways of conceptualizing the world but one scheme expressed differently. And if we cannot translate some alien noise-making behavior, then "we probably ought to hold that a form of activity that cannot be interpreted as language in our language is not speech behavior"(1984, 86). Thus, it is not coherent to suppose that there could be an alternative or alien conceptual scheme, and therefore the very notion is bankrupt. Davidson does not rest with this point, however, noting that "it comes to little more than making translatability into a familiar tongue a criterion of language-hood." He adds, "As fiat, this lacks the appeal of self-evidence." Davidson goes on to present two explicit arguments for his position, one of which goes as follows (the other will be discussed below). According to the Quinean model, a conceptual scheme is a language that "fits experience as a whole" and expresses "the totality of our beliefs." But as Davidson remarks, "the notion of fitting the totality of experience . . . adds nothing intelligible to the simple concept of being true" (1984, 194). Or, as we should say more carefully, to the concept of being *taken to be true*. To take L as the totality of one's beliefs is simply another way of saying, on this model, that a scheme is the set of sentences taken to be true (or largely true). In Davidson's eyes, it is this last point that really dooms the possibility of an alien conceptual scheme. For if a scheme is a set of declarative sentences taken to be true, then a totally alien scheme would have to be a set of sentences that are largely true but not translatable. According to Davidson's theory of meaning, however, this criterion is useless, for translation and (an assumption of) truth intertwine. That is, on Davidson's view, the question of whether there could be untranslatable sentences that we take to be true becomes the question of "how well we understand the notion of truth, as applied to a language, independent of the notion of translation" (1984, 194). The answer is that we have no such understanding. On Davidson's picture, our general notion of what is true cannot transcend the sum of what we can truly *assert*—in either our own language or any translatable language. Hence, it literally makes no sense to talk of true but untranslatable sentences, and thus "there is not much hope for a test that a conceptual scheme is radically different from ours if that test depends on the assumption that we can divorce the notion of truth from that of translation" (1984, 195).

I do not share Davidson's conviction that truth and translation cannot be understood apart from one another. But even if one rejects Davidson's arguments, there are still good reasons to abandon QM. I shall briefly rattle them off (acknowledging that those convinced by Davidson will see me as beating a dead horse—with the wrong sticks at that).[8] First, it is misleading, at best, to think of a conceptual scheme as essentially a language, especially when a language is thought of as a list of sentences under an interpretation (or as a function from such sentences to an interpretation). This picture of conceptual schemes is too simplified to be of much use: *our* language *is* vague and ambiguous, unlike L; *our* concepts intertwine and overlap in numerous and arcane ways. Second, a language isn't "the sum of declarative sentences I accept." Languages—if they must be looked at as sets of sentences at all—contain many types of sentences: sentences used to question and command, for instance. Surely such sentences are as equally important to the formation of a meaningful language as declarative sentences. Third, declarative sentences are what we *use* in expressing the propositions framed and structured by our conceptual scheme—they shouldn't be identified with those propositions. That would be to confuse *what is said* with what is used to say it. Fourth, even if we did take languages to be like *L* above, taking them to be conceptual schemes would imply that people who spoke the same "extensional" language would automatically share the same scheme. Yet this strikes me as quite implausible. A hinduist and myself may "assign the same extension" to the term "cow" and yet have radically different *concepts* of a cow. Thus, I do not find it plausible that an extensional interpretation is sufficient to fix meaning. Finally, even my own set of beliefs will doubtless contain contradictions, and surely my beliefs will contradict in countless ways with those of others. It follows that, on the Quinean model as I've understood it, conceptual schemes are seemingly doomed as inconsistent piles of sentences.

For all these reasons, the Quinean model of conceptual schemes is not, in the end, a happy one. Is the Kantian model then preferable? Not exactly, for that model sins in the other direction. Quine was *right* to emphasize that there is no clear-cut difference between "analytic" and "synthetic" truths, and (along with Kuhn) was *right* in emphasizing the important connection between scheme and language. In casting our gaze back upon the Kantian model, we should not ignore these lessons.

2.4   The Wittgensteinian Model

Something similar to the Quinean model of conceptual schemes is implicitly employed by most philosophers who currently use the term. Yet the field has not been totally won by the Quineans. There are signs that philosophers are reluctant to part completely with the Kantian legacy.

Hilary Putnam, to begin with, would appear to be of two minds when it comes to conceptual schemes. At first glance, one might count him as a loyal member of the Quinean camp. For he often takes schemes to be linguistic in nature and more than once has used the term "conceptual scheme" as interchangeable with "language."[9] In addition, he takes schemes as sentential and as "expressing the totality of our beliefs."[10] Thus he presumably accepts QM1. But he rejects QM3, for he is reluctant to part with the analytic/synthetic distinction and spurns as self-refuting the "incommensurability" that Kuhn and others embraced as following from the rejection of that distinction. The problem with such views, Putnam suggests, is that they conflate concept with conception; that is, they confuse our concept of x with our beliefs about x.

To the extent that the analytic/synthetic distinction is fuzzy, this distinction too is fuzzy; but all interpretation involves such a distinction, even if it is relative to the interpretation itself. . . . That conceptions differ does not prove the impossibility of ever translating anyone "really correctly" as is sometimes supposed; on the contrary, we could not say that conceptions differ and how they differ if we couldn't translate. (Putnam 1981, 116–117)

Putnam's point here is that some distinction, even a relative distinction, between what someone believes about xs (their conception of an x) and their concept of an x (what they mean by the word "x") is required for translation. When one translates a word, one is self-consciously attempting to capture the *concept* expressed by it. In many cases, it may be difficult to disentangle the other's beliefs about x from her concept of an x, but when one is engaged in translation, that is in fact what one is *trying* to do. The distinction between conception and concept may be fuzzy, but it is a distinction we have and, more important, *use* all the same. And since translation of another's speech or writing is necessary if we are to assess whether they are in agreement with us or not, some sort of distinction between our beliefs and concepts is necessary as well. In turn, this distinction between what we believe and what we mean gives rise to a corresponding distinction between statements true in virtue of the meanings involved (analytic statements) and statements true in virtue of how it is with the world (synthetic statements).

Putnam's point is reminiscent of a powerful metaphor of Wittgenstein's. According to Wittgenstein, our worldview is similar to a riverbed, where certain "hardened propositions" function as the bed of the river, acting as the form that contains and guides the mass of our ever-changing belief system. Yet, according to Wittgenstein, "The river-bed of thoughts may shift. But I distinguish between the movement of the waters on the river-bed and the shift of the bed itself; though there is not a sharp division between one or the other" (1969, 15e). In the course of our conceptual lives, we must, at any particular time, make a distinction between those parts of our conceptual scheme that are relatively unchanging and firm and act to guide the beliefs we form on a day-to-day basis and those beliefs themselves. But we need not think that the difference between these parts—between propositions that we take to be true in virtue of their concepts alone and propositions that are true or false in light of experience—as being a sharp and absolute difference. Just as the sides of the river determines its course, so the rushing waters of the river slowly alter the course of the river over time. Just as our beliefs change and alter, so do our concepts, and just as our concepts alter, so do our beliefs.

Wittgenstein often referred to these "riverbed" propositions as "grammatical" propositions. As Hans-Johann Glock has argued (1996), Wittgenstein believed that an identifying feature of these grammatical or conceptual propositions is the *normative* role they play within our worldview. A proposition is a conceptual truth, not because there is "some reality lying behind the notation, which shapes its grammar" (1958, sec. 562) but because we *use* that proposition as a standard of correct use (Glock 1996, 211). We share norms, in the form of propositions, on the basis of which we rule out other propositions as not making sense, as absurd or irrational. Of course, whether a proposition is or is not occupying a normative role isn't always clear, but a fuzzy distinction is still a distinction. And, as Glock notes, the distinction is clear enough to enable us to see a difference between changes in concepts (the riverbed) and changes in belief (the river). Simply put, a change involves a change in concept, in the meaning of certain expressions, just when the expressions in question can be employed meaningfully in ways that once made no sense or when we can no longer use them to make statements that at one point did make sense (Glock 1996, 212). Such changes involve a shift in the normative status of the expression.

On this picture, there are conceptually true, or analytic, propositions, but a proposition's having this status is due not to the intrinsic nature of the proposition, but to the role the proposition plays in our life. Late in part 1 of the *Investigations* (1958), Wittgenstein considers a variation of chess that prescribes that the kings must be used for drawing lots before the game begins. Such a rule does not strike us as essential to chess, but yet, Wittgenstein's interlocutor notes, games are defined by rules, and hence such a rule, if in place, must be essential to that game.

What objection might one make to this? That one does not see the point of the prescription. Perhaps as one wouldn't see the point either of a rule by which each piece had to be turned round three times before one moved it. If we found this rule in a board game we should be surprised and should speculate about the purpose of the rule. (1958, sec. 567)

So I am inclined to distinguish between the essential and the inessential in a game too. The game, one would like to say, has not only rules but a *point*. (1958, sec. 564)

In both games and conceptual schemes, one finds rules that strike us as essential or as inessential, and in both, we can ultimately distinguish these rules only by looking at the point, purpose, or role the rule or concept plays in context.

These reflections encourage a view of conceptual schemes that lies somewhere between our two paradigms. Whether such a view is tenable is not immediately clear, of course, but these authors' remarks raise the possibility of a neo-Kantian or Wittgensteinian view, one that retains what was valuable in the original Kantian metaphors without abandoning what is of use in Quine's view. Such a middle path is attractive, but some crucial questions have yet to be discussed. For this, I turn to Strawson.

In various works but most explicitly in *Analysis and Metaphysics* (1992), Strawson has hinted at a view of conceptual schemes that bears an important relation to the Kantian model. According to Strawson, philosophy in general is the work of trying to understand what he calls "basic" concepts. A concept is basic in this sense when "it is one of a set of general, pervasive, and ultimately irreducible concepts or concept-types which together form a structure—a structure which constitutes the framework of our ordinary thought and talk" (1992, 24). The types of concepts Strawson has in mind are neither the most simple nor those to which every other concept can somehow be "reduced." Rather, the idea is that basic concepts are those whose grasp are presupposed in our employing a large extent of our other, more specific concepts. These concepts are *highly general,* presumably, in that many other concepts naturally fall under them without them falling naturally under any other concept. And they are *irreducible,* Strawson says, in that they "cannot be defined away, without circularity, in terms of those other concepts to which [they] are necessarily related" (1992, 23). I would add that such concepts are *significant* in that they play important roles within our conceptual scheme. A concept will not be basic, in other words, unless it matters to us, that is, unless going without such a concept would severely limit and reshape our conceptual life to the point of unrecognizability.

Since it would be absurd to attempt any exhaustive investigation of such concepts in this context, let me simply note that concepts that fit the above criteria can arguably be said to fall into three natural categories. First, there are those general concepts that, as Kant rightly noted, are employed throughout every facet of our sensory experience: the concepts of substance, of space and of time (or perhaps I should say the one concept of space-time). Such concepts are presupposed in our daily dealings with the physical furniture of the world. Second, there are those concepts that rest at the heart of the judgments we make, broadly speaking, about the social realm, e.g., our concepts of morality, person, and gender. Third, there are those concepts that Wittgenstein called "formal" concepts, which are generally applicable in an even more radical sense. One's concept of identity, for instance, is going to play a large part in determining not only how one thinks about the world but also how one thinks about one's thinking about the world, as will the concepts of composition, fact, and object. In sum, all three types of concepts are presupposed when we apply more specific concepts in the nitty-gritty of life, from judging that the clerk behind the counter is the same person we spoke to yesterday to wondering where to plant the rose bush. In a very obvious sense, they limit and structure the variety of our judgments about the world. We think and talk in the way we do partly in virtue of the basic concepts we implicitly possess.

Strawson's basic concepts are therefore similar in some ways to Kant's categorical concepts. For in both cases, it is precisely in virtue of a certain ubiquity of presupposition that a concept can be plausibly said to "structure" our thoughts and statements. It is because they are presupposed by so much of our thought that basic concepts are properly called "basic." This suggests understanding a conceptual scheme as a framework of interrelated concepts, the most essential nodes of which are basic concepts of the sort just described. I have decided, somewhat reluctantly, to call this the *Wittgensteinian model* (WM). I am reluctant because Wittgenstein didn't discuss "models" or theories per se, and furthermore, not all of the view's components would Wittgenstein accept. Nonetheless, I hope that the reader will agree that the name suits the model in more ways than it doesn't suit it.

WM1   *Conceptual schemes are schemes of concepts.*

According to WM, one's conceptual scheme is not the totality of sentences one accepts as true. Rather, it is a network of general and specific concepts used in the propositions we express in language and in thought. The concept of a concept being employed here is a functional one. Concepts are whatever composes the propositional content of our assertions and beliefs. Therefore, to have or grasp a concept involves being able to use it when asserting or believing. To have the concept of a tree is to be able to pick out trees from nontrees, to make judgments about trees, and to understand at least some of the consequences of such judgments. But this functional characterization of concepts does not itself imply any particular ontological view about what plays the role of concepts. That is, none of this entails any particular ontology of concepts: they might be abstract entities, dispositions, or simply general terms under something called an "interpretation." Finally, the present model does not identify schemes with languages. Yet it is consistent with, although it does not demand, taking these networks of concepts as essentially depending on or connected to language.

WM2   *Schemes differ to the degree that they do not share basic concepts.*

Following Strawson, we can say that basic concepts are those concepts whose grasp are presupposed in our employing the large extent of our other, more specific concepts. Just as my body has parts not crucial to its existence and games may have rules not essential to their existence (given their point), so my overall conceptual scheme is composed of many nonbasic concepts (in my conceptual scheme, for instance, the concept of formica is relatively unessential). Basic concepts are irreducible, highly general, and play a significant role in our conceptual life. Actually, I think that the advocate of WM could just as well claim that any difference in concepts causes *some* change in the scheme, which is surely true. Even so, it is basic concepts which seem to really matter for individuation of a scheme, for their pervasive presupposition entails that even a slight change in a basic concept will ripple throughout the scheme as a whole.

WM3   *Conceptual schemes are consistent with nonsharp, fuzzy analytic/ synthetic and related distinctions.*

Our new model does require a distinction between form (concept) and content (belief), for WM holds that a scheme is a framework of concepts that we use to frame our beliefs. Thus it must be possible to discuss one's concepts and one's beliefs separately. This in turn naturally implies that there is a distinction between analytic and synthetic statements. However, as we saw Wittgenstein and Putnam claim above, there is no reason to see this distinction as sharp and absolute. One can maintain that there are some truths properly understood to be true in virtue of their component concepts, some truths true in virtue of the way the world is, and some truths (perhaps a great many, in fact) that do not determinably fall into either of the other two categories. Further, it seems possible to hold that which truths fall into which category (analytic, synthetic, indeterminate) changes over time. The distinction between the form and content of our scheme may be a fuzzy and indistinct moving target, shifting as our conceptual scheme changes and grows. But again, a fuzzy distinction is still a distinction.

WM4   *Schemes are only structurally foundationalist.*

According to the Kantian model, some set of categorical or basic concepts are absolutely basic. They are necessary for the application of any concepts whatsoever and therefore form a fixed and invariant foundation for our conceptual life. But according to WM, basic concepts are *not* absolutely basic. They are contextually basic—basic for a set of general and specific concepts *within a context.*[11] Within a particular historical context, certain concepts of ours will be foundational, that is, widely presupposed by other concepts, but this is consistent with acknowledging that changes in which concepts are basic, or changes in the nature of those concepts, can occur *over time.* The Wittgensteinian model takes schemes to be foundationalist in form but not in function.

Taken together, these views provide a substantial theory of conceptual schemes, according to which more than one set of basic concepts is possible. It is not necessarily a pluralist theory (that is, an absolutist metaphysician might adopt it if she wished), but it is certainly friendly to pluralist intuitions, and as we shall see, it is able to overcome certain problems its immediate predecessor could not.

WM also allows for a whole spectrum of pluralist views, depending on one's attitude toward different conceptual schemes. For instance, there is this contrast:

ACTUAL PLURALISM   *There is more than one conceptual scheme.*

MODAL PLURALISM   *It is possible for there to be more than one conceptual scheme.*

Actual and modal pluralism are consistent, but modal pluralism is a weaker thesis, for it is also consistent with the denial of actual pluralism, i.e., it is compatible with the idea that there is only one actual conceptual scheme. Both actual and modal pluralism can in turn be divided into subgroups. Actual pluralisms will vary depending on the number of different conceptual schemes believed to exist. And modal pluralisms will differ due to the type of modality involved. Hence,

STRONG MODAL PLURALISM   *It is physically possible that there is more than one conceptual scheme.*

WEAK MODAL PLURALISM   *It is* only *logically possible that there is more than one conceptual scheme.*

In the vocabulary of possible-worlds modal semantics, a state of affairs is *physically possible* if, and only if, it obtains in any possible world where the laws of nature are identical to the laws of nature at the actual world. A state of affairs is *logically possible* if there is at least one possible world where it obtains. A state of affairs is *only logically possible*, however, if, and only if, it is logically but not physically possible that it obtain. In other words, a state of affairs is only logically possible when it could obtain only if the laws of nature were different from what they actually are. So weak modal pluralism forms one boundary of a spectrum: according to weak modal pluralism, conceptual perspectives, different ways of ordering the world, are *only logically possible*. Yet, as weak as it is, weak modal pluralism is still opposed to absolutism. According to the latter view, there can be one and only one true account of the world. The truths of the world are unique and absolute.

WM also suggests a certain account of metaphysical investigation. R. G. Collingwood once proclaimed, "Metaphysics is the attempt to find out what absolute presuppositions have been made by this or that person or group of persons, on this or that occasion or group of occasions, in the course of this or that piece of thinking" (1940, 47). This picture of the metaphysical enterprise is similar to that suggested by Strawson, by Wittgenstein, and, in turn, by the metaphysical pluralist. For on such views, the metaphysician will naturally look toward what I've called *contextually basic* concepts, those concepts that, as Collingwood implies, are "absolute" not in the sense of being fixed for every thinker but in the sense of being presupposed by the lion's share of one's thought in a particular historical circumstance. Metaphysics, on such a view, is an investigation of the presuppositions of our conceptual situation in the world. Yet as we shall see in the next chapter and again in section 6.6, where I shall discuss the nature of metaphysics in general, this cannot be the whole story; metaphysical investigation is not purely descriptive; it extends our concepts, as well as describing them.

2.5   The Very Idea

So goes the view of conceptual schemes that I will adopt in this book. Obviously there is more to say about conceptual schemes, but as with many issues related to the main theme of this book, pursuing them further would simply be impractical. Yet I certainly need to address one more issue at least. I shall close this chapter with a discussion of how WM fares against Davidson's arguments against conceptual schemes.

Let us begin with his argument, summarized above, that the notion of a conceptual scheme implies that we "divorce truth from translation." Again, the point is that according to QM, a scheme is a set of declarative sentences taken to be true. Hence an alien scheme, that is, a conceptual scheme wholly distinct from ours, would be a scheme that is "largely true but not translatable." But Davidson argues that our best understanding of how translation works (his understanding, naturally) rules out this possibility, because translation and truth are conceptually intertwined.

In response, one might first challenge the assumption that Davidson's theory of meaning is the correct one. But the advocate of WM needn't do so. Instead, one need only point out that on WM, conceptual schemes are *not sets of declarative sentences but networks of concepts*. It follows that an alien scheme will not be a set of sentences taken to be "largely true" and that the argument will fail to connect.

The argument above is intended by Davidson to tell against the notion of a completely alien conceptual scheme—one which, in his words, is "completely untranslatable." He also argues against the notion of a partially alien, that is, partially translatable, scheme. Davidson presents this second argument as resting on his principle of charity. When engaging in what he calls "radical translation," Davidson argues that one must start with the assumption that there is widespread agreement between oneself and the speakers whose speech is being translated. One must assume, in other words, that most of the beliefs of the speakers are true. Charity with regards to belief is a precondition of understanding; hence, as Davidson likes to put it, belief and meaning are intertwined. Davidson argues that we are therefore never warranted in taking some alien conceptual scheme to be partially untranslatable:

> If we choose to translate some alien sentence rejected by its speakers by a sentence to which we are strongly attached on a community bias, we may be tempted to call this a difference in schemes; if we decide to accommodate the evidence in other ways, it may be more natural to speak of a difference of opinion. But when others think differently from us, no general principle . . . can force us to decide that the difference lies in our beliefs rather than in our concepts. (1984, 197)

In other words, there is nothing that forces us to say that an anomaly in translation is a matter of their believing differently as opposed to their using different concepts. Davidson concludes that no clear meaning can be given even to the notion of a partly translatable but distinct conceptual scheme, because it is always possible to conclude that the aliens in question share our scheme but have different beliefs than us.

It seems to me that this argument involves something of a non-sequitur. Davidson's argument rests on the premise that belief and meaning are interdependent because of the so-called "principle of charity." And indeed, it does seem that to evaluate the meanings of an alien set of sentences, we must presuppose some overlapping area of agreement with regard to belief. Further, let us suppose that this itself implies (and I am not sure that it does) that there is no clear difference between ascriptions of false beliefs and ascriptions of different concepts. From the premise that there is no clear difference between such cases, it does not follow that we would *never* be justified in holding that some speaker is employing some concepts distinct from our own. Simply because it will be indeterminate in a large range of cases whether to ascribe a false belief to the speaker instead of a different concept, it does not follow that *all* cases are indeterminate.

It is perfectly possible for the advocate of WM to allow for considerable entanglement between belief and meaning. But we shouldn't allow such entanglement to blind us to the fact that we are perfectly capable of *abstracting, for purposes of philosophical elucidation,* our beliefs from our concepts and discussing them, if somewhat artificially, in isolation from one another. Just as we can discuss syntax separately from semantics, knowing full well all the time that the two are inseparable in any language, so we may, as I have above, discuss many facets of our beliefs or concepts in isolation from one another.

This is a good point at which to emphasize that according to my understanding, our conceptual scheme is only one element of a *worldview*. A worldview, as I'm using the word, is an organic whole whose parts—one of which is what I'm calling a conceptual scheme—can best be understood in relation to their functions inside that whole. For example, as the Quinean model suggests, one's concepts are formed together with the beliefs that one has about various issues, and vice versa. Inquiry into what concepts one might possess and inquiry into what beliefs one might have are best handled together. And yet beliefs and the concepts that travel with them are not the only elements of a worldview. Surely James was right in saying, "We plunge forward into the field of fresh experience with the beliefs our ancestors and we have made already and these determine what we notice; what we notice determines what we do; what we do again determines what we experience; so from one thing to another" (1907, 115). Like our eyes, our worldview is a complex system with various components, each of which must work together if we are to see anything at all. Our worldview includes not only our *beliefs and the concepts we employ in forming our beliefs, but the interests we have that help explain why we have those concepts, the values that guide those interests, and the underlying practices and capacities that limit and define our cognitive production and intake.* A worldview is what Wittgenstein sometimes called a "form of life."

To return to the main thread of my argument, I have now shown that WM is immune from the two arguments Davidson has made against conceptual schemes. Yet this is not quite satisfactory, for there remains the root intuition *behind* Davidson's arguments. Davidson summarizes his most general point or intuition this way:

> The dominant metaphor of conceptual relativism, that of differing points of view, seems to betray an underlying paradox. Different points of view make sense, but only if there is a common co-ordinate system on which to plot them; yet the existence of a common system belies the claim of dramatic incomparability. (1984, 184)

For Davidson, who has the Quinean model in mind, the "common co-ordinate system" must be a language, for language, he says, is necessary for thought, or in any event, necessary for the type of thought required for formulating networks of concepts (1984, 185). He identifies conceptual schemes with languages. Yet one needn't do so in order to make the point; all that is needed is the truism that languages necessarily reflect or express their conceptual schemes. Davidson could simply ask us to consider the alleged possibility of an alien conceptual scheme expressed in a language radically different from and incompatible with our own. Either we can translate that language into our own or we cannot. If we can, then that language is not actually operating with a different set of concepts but with the same concepts expressed differently. But if we can't translate the language, then according to Davidson, we have no reason to think that the noises or marks made by the aliens actually express concepts at all.

To begin with, the argument rests on a verificationist assumption. Essentially, Davidson's question is this: what situation would verify the existence of an alternative conceptual scheme? The reply: no such situation is possible. Hence, since we could never verify the existence of an alternative scheme, no alternative schemes are possible, and the idea itself is worth dismissing. Let us think about this for a moment. Suppose that it is true that we couldn't verify whether some alien behavior by creatures from Mars was their expression of a different conceptual scheme than our own. Suppose that we could never possess such verification. Why should this prove that no alternative schemes are possible? Admittedly, we cannot "rise above" our own concepts and see what the world might be like for someone who employs different concepts. But this amounts to little more than saying that we can't conceptualize the world except with our concepts—a point that hardly justifies thinking that there are no other concepts available. That would be analogous to saying that there is nothing that it is like to be a bat, since there is no way for us to verify that there is some way of experiencing the world, distinct from our own, that the bat enjoys and we do not (Nagel, 1974). In general, we can conceive *that* certain general types of states of affairs exist (or possibly exist) without knowing anything about them in detail—even without being *able* to know about them in detail. Nagel's differing types of conscious experience is one example. More generally still, we can conceive of there being true propositions that, because of a lack of cognitive development, we are unable to even entertain. Obviously, no examples are possible, but nonetheless, *that* there are such propositions certainly is possible. In the same vein, one can imagine *that* there are sets of concepts different from our own, even if (necessarily) one cannot say anything about what those concepts are.

But we can even do better than this when it comes to alternative conceptual schemes. We need not hang our hat on antiverificationism. We can, in addition, extrapolate from past experiences and thereby make the possibility of alternative conceptual schemes comprehensible.[12] The point is a simple one. Based on past experience, we know that new concepts are constantly coming into use: consider, for instance, the variety of new concepts available to us that were not available to ancient cultures. Further, since human cognitive capacities are limited (and memories short), old concepts are routinely forgotten and laid aside. Consequently, the ancients had concepts that we do not. There is in turn every reason to suspect that in the far off future, there shall be buckets of concepts radically distinct from our own and, further, that the users of those concepts may lack many of the concepts we take for granted.

What's more, Davidson's dilemma ignores the fact that *understanding is a matter of degree*. All of us have had the experience of understanding *some* of what a friend, professor, or speaker of another language was trying to communicate to us, while not being quite able to grasp all of what was being said. Further, translators are certainly familiar with being unable to find quite the right word or even series of words in English (or whatever language) with which to match words from another tongue. Harré and Krausz report, for instance, that "Japanese first person pronouns cannot be rendered without remainder by the English 'I' since there is no pronoun in Japanese which does not index a speech-act with the social position of the speaker, vis-à-vis hearer or counter-speaker" (1996, 51). Yet English speakers can recognize that certain words are being used functionally as pronouns without being able to capture quite the full concept the Japanese speaker will express when using that word. Indeed, we can often identify overlapping—if distinct—concepts by their function within their respective schemes. That is, as Rescher (1980, 328) has noted, we can classify others' speech acts as functionally equivalent to certain speech acts of ours without being able to say exactly what they mean, just as an ancient Roman coin can be seen as money even though it is impossible for us to guess its intended value. We do this by appealing to the other aspects of the aliens' behavior besides their speech: how they physically react to certain situations or what tools they might use or how they might use them. Through such methods we might arrive at the conclusion that the aliens have some concepts that perform some of the same jobs as certain of our concepts but that remain divergent from ours in their scope, the normative implications of their use, or the relative centrality of their place within the aliens' conceptual scheme. So someone who understands both languages or can employ both schemes may be able to get some idea across to me as to what is going on in the aliens' lives. But while such a person might herself fully understand certain concepts, she will be unable to completely convey that understanding to me unless I also begin to share that scheme, learn that language, experience that worldview.

In short, the model of conceptual schemes I have been defending does not entail that different conceptual schemes must be "incommensurable." Schemes are incommensurable only to the degree to which they do not share concepts, basic concepts in particular. Of course, such distinctness is not ruled out by WM. Yet, according to WM, adherents of different schemes need not be unintelligible to each other across the board, since, as I've just been arguing, distinct concepts can overlap. And if concepts can overlap, then so can conceptual schemes. In the next chapter, I shall dig deeper into this issue to see how a shared, overlapping concept can be extended in radically different directions.

3

Extending Our Worldview

The movement of reality is mirrored in the fluidity of concepts.
Max Horkheimer

3.1 Concepts: Two Pictures

Being human means being situated—not just physically but conceptually. Thought is always internal to a network of concepts. In chapter 1, I called this content relativism, the view that propositions contain an implicit "index" or reference to a conceptual scheme. Of course, propositions do not literally have secret markers; they don't wear invisible dog tags that say "I am the proposition that snow is white, if lost, return me to conceptual scheme C." The point is that our assertions and thoughts can be understood only by reference to the network of concepts out of which they emerge. In other words, the truth conditions of propositions are internal to a conceptual scheme. Yet that conceptual scheme itself is not something stamped upon us, immune from change. It emerges from the historical context of our lives. And there is or could be more than one context, even a plurality of different contexts—of different conceptual schemes and worldviews.

I ended the last chapter by arguing that conceptual schemes should be understood along Wittgensteinian lines. This view allows for distinct schemes to be partially commensurable; I can extend my conceptual scheme until my worldview overlaps with yours. On this view, schemes are structured around certain "contextually basic" concepts. These concepts are basic in that they are ubiquitously presupposed throughout much of our dealing with the world. So if we wish to understand the pluralist perspective, and in particular how conceptual schemes can change and overlap, we need to understand how these ideas play out at the level of individual concepts. Specifically, we need an explanation of what concepts must be like if they are to function in the way demanded by WM.

First, a word about what is meant by the word "concept" in general. Essentially, I shall continue to assume the minimal concept of a concept introduced in the last chapter, according to which concepts are the constituents of propositions, whatever they turn out to be. Concepts compose our thoughts; in short, a concept is a particular way of thinking about something or other. So to *have a concept* involves understanding or "seeing" something in a certain way, and moreover it implies the possession of certain abilities. To have the concept of a dog, for example, is to be able to pick dogs out from other animals, to be capable of understanding judgments about dogs, and to be capable of understanding at least some of the consequences of such judgments. Therefore, we can usefully distinguish concepts in terms of what Christopher Peacocke calls their "possession conditions" (1992). To use a simple example of Peacocke's, the conditions under which one could be said to truly possess the concept of logical conjunction are when one is compelled without further evidence, to infer p, q from p & q and vice versa (1992, 6). Similarly, it is also possible to discuss the conditions under which a concept is correctly applied—its application conditions, in other words. To keep with the same example, the concept of conjunction is correctly applied when one, naturally and without the aid of further evidence, infers p, q from p & q and vice versa. Obviously, application conditions and possession conditions are intrinsically connected. Trivially, one possesses the concept F when one can correctly apply F, and one can't correctly apply a concept unless one possesses, or grasps, that concept. To grasp a concept is just to know how to apply it correctly, and to apply it correctly entails that one grasps it.[1]

Broadly speaking, there have been two dominant pictures of concepts in the twentieth century, what I will call the *crystalline* and *fluid* pictures of concepts. It is perhaps roughly true that the crystalline picture is favored by absolutists and the fluid picture by pluralists. But I won't argue that subscribing to one or the other of the pictures automatically entails that you are an absolutist or a pluralist.[2] Philosophers are interested in concepts for all sorts of reasons, including reasons that have little to do with the present debate. I am interested in the more specific question of what sort of account of concepts is implied by the version of metaphysical pluralism developed in the last two chapters.

The more traditional of our two pictures holds that *concepts are like crystal*: rigid, pure, and transparent, with sharp edges and definite borders.[3] On this view, each concept must, by its very nature, have an absolutely determinate use in all *possible* cases in which it could apply. This picture is associated with the work of the early Wittgenstein but, even more paradigmatically, with Frege:

> A definition of a concept (of a possible predicate) must be complete; it must unambiguously determine, as regards any object, whether or not it falls under that concept. . . . We may express this metaphorically as follows: a concept must have a sharp boundary. (Frege 1952, 159)

For Frege, a concept (or its use) is "absolutely determinate" when its boundaries are always and everywhere precise. It is important to note that the requirement is not only universal but modal. That is, a concept must be determinant enough so that for any actual *or possible object*, it will either apply or not apply to that object, regardless of whatever other facts may apply. This is the sense in which concepts, like crystals, are rigid and pure. But they are also transparent, for to grasp a concept, to satisfy its possession conditions, is to know how the concept should be applied in all possible future cases. Thus the crystalline metaphor is at the heart of the widespread view that to understand a concept is to know the *necessarily necessary and sufficient conditions for its application*. To grasp the concept of a bachelor is to know not only that all bachelors are unmarried males and that all unmarried males are bachelors but also that there *could* be no situation in which a married man is a bachelor. To grasp a concept like bachelor, the crystalline picture of concepts suggests, is to know its application conditions in all possible worlds.

Motivations for adopting the crystalline picture can no doubt vary considerably, but here are two of the more prominent. First, there is simple intuition. We can share concepts, for example, concepts of what it is to be a dog or a desk or a successful baseball player. If so, then there is one concept that we have, and this shared concept must be "the" concept of a dog. But how could it make sense to talk of "the" concept of a dog unless there were definite criteria separating dogs from nondogs that we recognize? As Frege (1952, 159) argued, concepts can seem like closed circles: there could be no concept of a dog unless there were sharp lines separating what that concept applies to and what it does not. Second, there is the theoretical consideration, again due to Frege and the early Wittgenstein, that language—the medium by which we express our concepts—is essentially a truth-functional calculus. The meaning of propositional expressions (such as "There is a dog in the trash or a burglar in the yard") derives from the meaning of those expressions' more basic parts, that is, from the concepts of "dog," "yard," etc., along with the truth-functional operator "or." Hence, if concepts were not determinate, then the propositions they make up could never be determinate either. But the fact that we take our propositions as either true or false suggests that our concepts must be determinate; otherwise, again, how could propositions admit of only two truth values as they obviously do?

The crystalline picture doesn't require that one's actual application of a given concept be as pure and determinate as the concept itself. The traditionalist can acknowledge as well as anyone that our language is rife with ambiguous, vague, and imprecise applications of concepts. Of course, this fact demands an explanation, and broadly speaking, traditionalists have accounted for it in two sorts of ways. First, one might hold, as Frege seemed to, that due to the sloppiness of our thinking, the determinacy of concepts is an imperfectly reached ideal. In effect, the point is normative: we *ought* to be thinking perfectly determinately; truly legitimate conceptualization is determinate and precisely bounded, and to the extent to which our thinking meets these conditions, we are thinking rightly. Alternatively, one might say (as the early Wittgenstein apparently did) that our concepts actually do embody such determinacy now, but it is hidden from us, beneath the surface of language. This second sort of explanation is consistent with the idea that concepts are actually properties out in the world—properties whose true natures are obscured as often as they are mirrored by our thought. On either explanation, the bottom line is that legitimate concepts are determinate concepts. The point is not only that we *can* (at least sometimes) grasp such concepts but also that we always *should*. The norms of reason demand that our thought mirror as much as possible the crystalline nature of reality.

According to the crystalline picture of concepts, the job of philosophical analysis of some particular concepts is to state the necessary and sufficient conditions for the application of those concepts—to capture the essence those concepts express, in other words. The essence of an *F* is the property that makes an *F* what it is and that separates it from everything else. So in stating the necessary and sufficient conditions for the concept of an *F*, one is revealing the essence of being an *F*. Or as I might also put it, to adopt the crystalline picture of concepts is to understand that there is a unique and common property shared by everything which falls under the concept of an *F*, that there is an essence to being an *F* that determines absolutely whether the concept does or does not apply to it.

The crystalline picture of concepts appeals to the eye with its fine lines and brilliant reflective surfaces. But it does not fit well with the pluralist Wittgensteinian Model of conceptual schemes, according to which concepts can shift, change, and overlap. Accordingly, pluralism is more naturally roped to what we might call the fluid picture of concepts. On this second view, concepts are not "absolutely determinate" closed circles, but elastic and flexible. Concepts on this view are more like sculpting clay. Unlike crystal, which breaks easily, you can stretch and pull a piece of clay in radically different directions before it tears apart. Concepts too are always subject to radical changes in shape.

Two elements of this fluid picture of concepts bear special comment. First, the possession and application conditions of concepts need not be absolutely determinate. Here again Wittgenstein is the main advocate, although now, of course, in the later stage of his work:

Frege compares a concept to an area and says that an area with vague boundaries cannot be called an area at all. This presumably means that we cannot do anything to it.—But is it senseless to say: "Stand roughly here"? (1958, sec. 71)

The point is that imprecise, indeterminate uses of language are employed by us all the time during our daily life. In contrast to his earlier self, who, with Frege, worried that indeterminate concepts could not be used to communicate, the later Wittgenstein simply asks us to "look and see" that we actually do use such concepts every day. His most famous example, one that we will spend considerable time on in the next section, is the notion of a game. There simply seems to be no "common thread" that runs through all our applications of that concept that would tie all games together. There is nothing that is the essence of a game, and hence it has no absolutely determinate application conditions. As we shall see, there are cases where an activity is neither determinately a game or not a game. And yet clearly we can and do use the concept of a game.

A second way in which concepts can be fluid is by being incomplete or open in their *future* application. Suppose that a chair seems to disappear and reappear before our eyes, or that it grows, or that it moves by itself.

> What are we to say now? Have you rules ready for such cases—rules saying whether one may use the word "chair" to include this kind of thing? But do we miss them when we use the word "chair"; and are we to say that we do not really attach any meaning to the word, because we are not equipped with rules for every possible application of it? (Wittgenstein 1958, sec. 80)

But, of course, words like "chair" *do* have a meaning, even though the future application of the concept is open-ended, not closed. As Robert Fogelin has remarked (1996, 50), the later Wittgenstein dismisses his earlier demand that concepts behave with the "crystalline purity of logic," saying instead that such purity "was not the result of an investigation, but a requirement" (1958, sec. 107). In other words, the later Wittgenstein not only rejected the crystalline picture of our thought, he rejected the norms that gave that picture its urgency.

Anyone committed to the Wittgensteinian model of conceptual schemes will naturally find the fluid picture of concepts more attractive than its traditional counterpart. According to WM, the relatively firm bed of our concepts can shift and change over time in response to the rushing waters of experience. Thus WM implies that individual concepts themselves cannot be always and everywhere determinate but must instead be open to future change and alteration.

It is tempting to describe this fluid picture of concepts as implying that every concept is vague, but although that description is not completely off base, and while it is certainly hinted at by Wittgenstein himself, it would ultimately be unhappy for several reasons. First, vagueness, like precision, is a relative matter. There is little point in calling, e.g., a measurement precise unless we know what standard of precision is being applied. So there is little point in calling concepts vague unless we specify the standard by which we are comparing them. Second, "vague" often has associated with it a strong pejorative force according to which to be vague is to be in a muddle, to lack understanding. But in taking concepts to be flexible and fluidlike, the pluralist is not saying that we are confused about our concepts. Rather, the point is that concepts are not absolutely determinate or closed: they do not have a fixed use in every possible situation. This does not imply, however, that no concepts have determinate uses in all *actual* situations. Some concepts may be perfectly determinate in actual situations but not in all possible situations.

Minimally speaking, and independently of its pejorative force, a concept is vague when there are actual cases wherein it is neither true nor false that the concept applies. To put it differently, a concept is vague when there are actual disagreements over its application even when both of the usages in question are in equal accordance with past usage. The pluralist will take it that many concepts are vague in precisely this way. But while all vague concepts are examples of what I'm calling fluid concepts, not all fluid concepts are vague. For the pluralist, concepts are also flexible; they are subject to *possible* extension in the face of unforeseen circumstances. Hence, *there can be irresolvable disagreements over how to apply any concept.* In a sense, concepts are therefore always possibly vague in a nonpejorative sense; they have what Waismann called an "open texture."[4]

So on the picture of concepts as fluid, concepts are subject to a possible extension of use. Of course, the sense of "possible" involved here may vary from concept to concept, even when we are restricting our interest to basic metaphysical concepts. That is, it may be that for some concepts, irresolvable disagreements over applications may be "right around the corner" so to speak; such disagreements are not only logically and physically possible but also quite plausible, even if not actual as of yet. On the other hand, for some concepts, such disagreements may be only logically possible (see section 2.4). Nonetheless, even on its weakest interpretation, the metaphor of fluidity implies, among other things, that the search for the essence or common property expressed by a concept is futile. On such a picture, there is no demand for a property shared by all things that could fall under the concept (although the picture need not rule out the possibility of such properties).

Conceptual fluidity does not sit well with another implication of the traditional picture of metaphysical concepts, according to which it makes literal sense to talk about "the" concept of something or other: *the* concept of truth or *the* concept of knowledge or *the* concept of an object. To adopt such a view is to buy into what Paul Moser has called "the myth of the definite article" (1993, 153 ff). Since, on the pluralist view, it is always possible for our metaphysical concepts to diverge in that there can be cases where inconsistent applications are equally correct, it is always possible that there will be two or more equally legitimate concepts of an F. This, of course, does not mean that we cannot use the definite article in conjunction with the word "concept." Just as it is harmless to refer to the president when it is understood that we mean the president of the United States or the president of the company, so it can be harmless to discuss the concept of an F. It is just that on the pluralist understanding, we should not take this literally, or absolutely, and infer that there (necessarily) can only be one "F-concept."

This ends my rough and ready introduction of the fluid picture of concepts assumed by metaphysical pluralism. The next step is to examine two specific ways in which our concepts actually are flexible in just the way envisaged by the fluid picture. In chapter 4, I'll apply these lessons to specific metaphysical concepts.

3.2   Conceptual Fluidity and Family Resemblance

As we've already noted, a paradigmatic example of what I've been calling a fluid concept is a "family resemblance" concept.[5] According to Wittgenstein (1958, secs. 67–71), the activities we group together under the word "game"—to cite his most notorious example—do not share some common property or properties; that is, there are no properties, other than the property of being a game, that all and only games have. Rather, what makes various activities games is a certain overlapping network of similarities. Just as all the members of a family can look like they are related without sharing any one feature in common (such as eye or hair color), every game shares some property with some other game, but there is no property that every game shares with every other game *and* with nothing else that isn't a game. Many games, but not all, involve competition (think of a child throwing a ball up against a wall), and many other activities that are not games (business, war) are competitive. Again, many games are recreational, but not all recreational activities are games. Some games involve teams, but many do not. Hence, a word like "game" cannot be defined by giving a unique set of necessary and sufficient conditions. Rather, "game" obtains its meaning by being used in reference to certain paradigmatic cases, such as baseball, and by being extended to other activities similar to baseball in some respects (Wittgenstein 1958, sec. 71). But there is no principle that tells us how similar to baseball something must be in order to count as a game.

So we learn concepts like "game," and other arguably similar concepts like "art," "music," and "pornography," by extrapolating from paradigmatic examples and placing objects that are similar in certain respects under the same concept. Ironically, this definition of a family-resemblance concept seems itself to be a bit too fluid. After all, it is plausible to think that we learn *most* of our concepts, including many non-family-resemblance concepts, by extrapolating from paradigms or prototypes. Suppose for a moment that this is true. Is there anything else that we might say about family-resemblance concepts that would help us to extrapolate in the right direction from our paradigm example of "game"?

There is. When we are concerned with a concept that is correctly applied just when it is similar to a paradigm, the following two questions are important: What similarities do we focus upon? Which examples do we take as paradigmatic? Consider a concept like gold. In the case of the concept gold, Putnam has argued that because of the "division of linguistic labor" the answer to both questions lies with the experts.[6] Roughly speaking, the point is that with "natural kind" concepts like gold or water, we defer to those in our society whom we take to be knowledgeable about the inner nature of gold or water. If these experts determine that anything that has atomic number 79 is identical to gold, then even if we came across a community that also used the word "gold" to apply to any soft, malleable yellow metal, if that metal doesn't have the same molecular makeup, we won't say that it is gold. We apply the word "gold" with the intention of applying it to the same sorts of stuff to which the experts apply it; hence our concept of gold is the concept of stuff that has the same inner nature as the paradigmatic examples of gold, as determined by the experts. The result is that the division of linguistic labor determines for us how similar things must be in order to be gold and what counts as paradigmatic gold in the first place.

Concepts like game are much more slippery. In particular, it would seem that in the case of concepts like game, we can and do appeal to *different* paradigms when deciding whether to apply the word. The division of linguistic (or conceptual) labor does not nail down what is to count as a paradigm. This is what I shall take as the most important feature of family-resemblance concepts (for our purposes, anyway).

It is useful to have an example. Suppose two amateur anthropologists, call them Smith and Johnson, visit a remote community of island-dwelling people. We can imagine that Smith and Johnson observe and record in their journal the following behavior during their visit:

The healthy adult Islanders form into two evenly sized groups. For a period of two hours, each group digs a hole in the earth, and throughout that time, each group tries to throw the dirt from their hole into the other group's hole. The groups themselves are specialized: some members of each group concentrate only on digging, some members only on throwing dirt into the other group's hole. Once the two hours are up, the holes are measured, and the group with the deepest hole celebrates. The members of the other group are seriously shamed, and must supply hefty amounts of food and tribute to the first group. The entire affair is conducted in utter seriousness, and angry shouting matches and even extreme physical violence often break out. Furthermore, there are clearly some sacred rituals involved; for example, prior to and after the digging, each group prays to their twin deities, who are generally depicted as bearing shovels and trowels. And all disputes are settled by the high shaman.

We can easily imagine our amateur anthropologists getting in a dispute over how to classify this behavior. Smith calls it a game: there are teams, she notes, and offense, and defense, and clear winning and losing. Johnson disagrees; it is a religious ritual, he insists, pointing out that it is taken very seriously, that it is not at all relaxing, that it involves sacred rituals, and that the whole affair is controlled by the shamans. He points out that it could very well be a religiously important enactment of the Islanders' creation myth.

Who is right? Are the Islanders playing a game or not? The answer is that both Smith and Johnson are right, for they are each appealing to different paradigms in explaining their decision. With a concept like game, there is no reason to think that our list of paradigmatic examples must overlap. It can therefore be indeterminate whether certain activities are games. Indeed, fanciful examples are not necessary. One need not look any further than the disputes that routinely spring up about what should be included in the Olympic Games. Is ballroom dancing, for example, a game or sport?[7]

Some might wish to conclude that Smith and Johnson are simply equivocating over the word "game"; thus, the Islanders' activity is a game on Smith's concept of a game but not on Johnson's. Yet this is surely incorrect, for Smith and Johnson presumably can understand each other very well. It would be more true to our actual practice to say that we share one very fluid concept of game rather than many very distinct concepts.[8] This is Wittgenstein's point when he says that we wish to apply "game" to all these phenomena, that we resist such compartmentalization of the concepts of game (1958, sec. 532). The reasons are clear enough: first, there is general agreement on the paradigmatic examples of games in a culture (even though, as with "gold" we don't have experts to consult), and second, our concept of a game is useful precisely because it is so elastic. It allows us to group many activities under one category for many different reasons: a useful feature indeed, given our penchant for inventing new activities to engage in.

So, on the one hand, we can acknowledge that there are cases where you and I can disagree about whether x is a game but both be correct, as in the above example. On the other hand, we needn't say that we are using distinct concepts of a game. We are each using a concept of a game that operates as a family-resemblance notion. Our concept of a game is a flexible concept par excellence. And this, in turn, means that when we do talk of "the" or "our" concept of a game, we are speaking of a nonabsolute, shifting target that can be applied in inconsistent ways, relative to different paradigms.

3.3   Conceptual Fluidity and Minimal Concepts

For our purposes, the importance of a concept like "game" (and other likely candidates for family resemblance, such as "art," "religion," and "philosophy") is that it can be both true and false that something is a game, depending on the paradigm one uses when applying or not applying the concept. And yet, unlike with the word "bank," we don't take disputes over how to apply the concept (such as the one I imagined occurring over the Islander example above) to be resolved by simply pointing out that the disputants are equivocating. Family-resemblance concepts are fluid but not ambiguous.

There is another phenomenon involving our concepts, similar to family resemblance, that points to the same result. As Paul Moser has noted, "People operating with different specific notions of X can still, however, understand and even intentionally use common conceptions of X generally characterized. We thus can talk intelligibly of various notions of some one thing (generally characterized)" (1993, 78). For example, Moser argues that two philosophers might have different "operative definitions" of epistemic justification and yet share a definition of that concept "generally characterized." In the most general sense, epistemic justification is that feature of beliefs, other than truth, that is desirable from the epistemic point of view, from which one is engaged in inquiry or seeking to know. In short, epistemic justification is that feature a belief must have in addition to truth if it is to count as knowledge.[9] Nonetheless, as anyone familiar with Anglo-American epistemology well knows, we can *extend* this generic concept of justification in different directions. A "reliabilist" takes a justified belief to be a reliably formed belief, a "coherentist" would claim that it is a belief that coheres with the believer's other beliefs, while a third epistemologist might claim that a justified belief is a belief for which the believer can defend with evidence or reasons. As those working in the epistemological trenches can verify, many of these specific (Moser would say "operative") concepts of justification cannot be made consistent with one another, and yet the participants in these debates, when employing these differing concepts, are not plausibly taken as simply equivocating over the word "justification." Their individual concepts of justification are linked in that they all merit the label of "justification-concept."

The point is that we often stretch concepts in incompatible directions. Beginning with a shared concept, we can extend it in different directions by narrowing or widening its application. The concept of mind is another example. The typical person who uses the word "mind" in everyday speech normally does not know very much about the mind or about our best theories concerning it. And yet the word certainly has a common meaning. Minimally speaking, a mind is simply something that thinks, feels, and has conscious experience. Yet more specific and robust concepts can also be used, both in everyday parlance as well as in philosophical discussion. In the introduction to a prominent collection of readings on the philosophy of mind, David Rosenthal writes, "Our commonsense picture of mind therefore involves components that pull in opposite directions. According to one, mind is a singularity in nature, discontinuous with all other natural processes; the other points instead to a conception of mind as intimately bound to, and dependent upon, various nonmental processes" (1991, 5). These extensions of our shared concept of mind (what Rosenthal is calling "our commonsense picture of mind") are not simply creations of the philosopher. They brush up against one another in the culture at large. A favorite example of mine is drawn from my own experience in the classroom. First-year philosophy students, when confronted with arguments for materialist views of mind for the first time, have sometimes tied themselves into knots by saying either in a paper or in class discussion, e.g. "My *brain* is just not a physical thing!" Of course, on the face of it, this is not a very plausible thing to say. It may even appear downright dim. And yet it is not as if the students in question do not know that the brain is a biological organ, as physical in nature as their left big toe. They clearly do know this. And the fact that such slips happen as often as they do rules out the possibility of simple dyslexia or some such. Rather, the explanation lies in the fact that we have at least two concepts of mind floating about in our cultural repertoire, and inconsistent concepts at that. On the one hand, we have the physical concept of mind inherited from the sciences. Hence speakers will actually use "brain" and "mind" as synonyms. All of us are familiar with phrases like "My brain is just not working today" or "What a brainy person you are!" On the other hand, there is also the dualistic concept of mind abstracted from religion: the mind is a nonphysical spiritual object of some sort. It is this concept that folks are using when they profess not to *understand* the idea that the mind can be completely described physically.

Yet users of these different concepts (such as the neuroscientist and the dualist philosopher) obviously can communicate with one another about minds. When the dualist philosopher and the neuroscientist debate about the mind, they neither are, nor take themselves to be, discussing *completely* different subjects; they are not simply equivocating over the word. They are employing different concepts of mind, and yet both concepts are clearly "mind concepts."

What makes all of our epistemologist's individual concepts of justification worth calling "concepts of justification" or both our neuroscientific and dualist concepts of mind "concepts of mind" is that they are all extensions of what I would call a *minimal concept* of epistemic justification or mind. A minimal concept of F is a concept whose ordinary use "floats free" of metaphysical questions (or most metaphysical questions) surrounding Fs. It is a way of thinking about something that is neutral with regard to issues about its ontological nature. In the example of the concept of mind, our minimal concept of mind is whatever it is that thinks and has experience. In contrast, what I will call a *robust concept* of F is a concept whose ordinary use consists of a commitment to some particular ontological view of Fs. Thus, a robust concept is a way of thinking about something that is not neutral with regard to questions about its ontological status. The Cartesian concept of mind, with its commitment to a nonphysical substance, is a comparatively more robust concept.

The minimal/robust distinction can be put in different ways. Put linguistically, the minimal sense of the word "F" does not commit the speaker to any particular ontological view on the nature of Fs. Put adverbially, to speak minimally about Fs, or to conceive of Fs minimally, is to remain mute on the subject of the ultimate nature of Fs. We can also capture the idea at the level of propositions: a proposition about Fs is minimal to the degree to which its truth or falsity does not depend on the resolution of ontological debates about Fs. True to the pluralist position I have been attempting to explain, I shall take all of these to be equally perspicuous ways of stating the same point.

As I understand it, the minimal/robust distinction, like the distinction between big and small, is comparative and a matter of degree. While for simplicity's sake I might talk about "the" minimal concept of mind or epistemic justification or identity, this should be understood as simplifying the fact that one's use of a concept is minimal relative to more robust possible applications of that same concept. Considered completely in the abstract, concept F_1 is more minimal than F_2 only if applications of F_2 entail (an implicit) application of F_1 but not vice versa. Similarly, F_1 is minimal relative to F_2 only if a statement of the possession conditions of F_2 entail the possession conditions of F_1 but not vice versa. But abstract descriptions are only so helpful. The point is that robust concepts (or comparatively more robust concepts) are naturally thought of as *enrichments* or *extensions* of their more minimal counterparts. This relation of enrichment is analogous to the realization of a function. It is as if the minimal concept of, e.g., mind describes a certain function: a mind is whatever thinks. Another relevant example would be the minimal concept of proposition I introduced in chapter 1: a proposition, I claimed, is whatever stands to asserting and denying as numbers stand to adding and subtracting. Or think of the concept of fact or even of concept itself; I have been intentionally employing minimal concepts throughout our discussion. If we think of minimal concepts as describing a function, then we can consider a robust concept as a way of thinking about how the function in question is instantiated or realized.

The analogy between the minimal/robust distinction and the function/realization distinction reveals another point as well. Consider two descriptions of the heart:

- The heart is what pumps the blood.
- The heart is that multichambered organ that propels blood through the body by alternating dilatations and contractions, the blood being received from the veins and returned through the arteries.

At first glance, we might say that the first description is "functional" and the second "structural," or a description of how that function is realized or instantiated. But the second description is itself functional relative to a more fine-grained chemical or even atomic description of the heart. Whether a description is functional is not absolute but a matter of how it is used in context in relation to other descriptions. The same holds when we are considering whether a particular assertion involves a minimal or robust concept. Whether we take an assertion like "The mind is the brain" or "The mind is independent of the body" to be employing a minimal or robust concept of mind depends on how that assertion is being used in context. If we use such expressions normatively, for instance, as laying down implicit rules for what it does and doesn't make sense to say or think, then it is reasonable to take them as employing (and defining) robust concepts of mind. But we might also take them, in the right context, as asserting certain truths about the mind, considered minimally.

These reflections bring out what is important about the minimal/robust distinction for pluralism. The pluralist will claim that minimal concepts can be enriched or extended in incompatible directions. Above, I suggested that this is precisely the case with the concepts of epistemic justification and mind. To anticipate, I shall argue in the next two chapters that the minimal concepts of object and truth are fluid in just the same way. But there is a difference between these examples. In the case of a concept like that of mind, one might agree that it is fluid without agreeing that each extension of the concept can be applied correctly in the actual world. With the concepts of object and truth, we shall see that this position is much less plausible. With highly abstract concepts, equally correct but inconsistent applications are intuitively coherent.[10]

But let's not get ahead of ourselves. Despite what I've said so far on the subject, some may insist that what I've called more robust concepts of mind are really just different beliefs about the mind. That is, the absolutist about concepts might try to acknowledge much of what I've said but simply recast it as differences over what a mind is. For both the dualist and the neuroscientist, our imaginary absolutist might say that there is one and only one concept of mind and perhaps that concept is just what I've said. A mind is whatever thinks. What I call differing robust concepts of mind are not differing concepts at all but differences about what this thing is that thinks—about the nature of the mind, in other words.

In response, it is tempting to simply point at our actual linguistic practice; surely we possess different concepts *and* different beliefs about the mind. But that is perhaps a less than persuasive answer. A better answer begins by simply admitting that the dispute between the dualist and the neuroscientist is a dispute about the mind. It is a dispute over the facts—which, as a matter of necessity, implies that the disputants share the same concept of mind. Yet it is also the case that our disputants do not share the same concept: as I just remarked, it is quite reasonable to believe that they do not mean exactly the same thing by "mind." What we wish to say, and what we should say, is this: *our neuroscientist and Cartesian friends both do and do not share the same concepts of mind!* To repeat, just as one and the same description can be both functional and structural, depending on the context in which it is expressed, so one and the same proposition can be composed of a concept that is both minimal and robust, depending on the context in which it is expressed. It is this fact that disposes us to think that the neuroscientist and the Cartesian (and the internalist and externalist in epistemology) are using the same concept *and* using different concepts. Rather than attempting to "explain this away," we should trust our intuitions, for this very contradiction points to the flexible nature of our thought.

Yet the fact that there is no *absolute* distinction between taking two disputants to be employing the same minimal concept and taking the same disputants to be employing different robust concepts does not entail that there is no distinction at all between these alternatives. This is exactly the point I made in the last chapter concerning differences between concepts and differences over beliefs. Again, just as there is no fixed, absolute dividing line between "analytic" and "synthetic" propositions, so there is no such line between disputes "over the facts" about, e.g., minds and disputes involving different concepts of mind. But this is not to deny the usefulness and importance of making such a distinction within a particular interpretative context, that is, at a particular moment of use. To realize, for instance, that there is no fixed line between what is part of the meaning of "chair" and our largely inarticulate knowledge about chairs is not to claim that we can't make such a distinction. Of course we can, and do, but how we do so and where we draw the line depend on the particulars of the situation at hand.

This distinction between minimal and robust concepts has several theoretical benefits. Most important, the distinction helps us to understand (together with family-resemblance concepts) the pluralist picture of concepts as fluid, and so in turn the central notion of content relativism itself. In particular, it helps us see what the pluralist means by saying that conceptual schemes can overlap or share content.

A metaphor is helpful here. Suppose that we are presented with a crudely drawn sketch—no more than a few rough lines. Imagine that we have two different artists "fill in" this sketch. In one sense, we would no doubt get two very different pictures. Now suppose that we ask which of these pictures is the *real* painting of the scene in the sketch. Obviously, there can be no answer. Both and neither are. Similarly, if I ask what is the sketch *really* a sketch of, we again cannot answer without appeal to a particular "filling in" of the rough lines of the sketch (whether real or only imagined).

Just as one sketch can be filled in in different but equally correct ways, so one concept—and by implication, one proposition—be employed or used in more than one correct way. Further, in the way in which two painters can paint the same scene differently or fill out the same sketch differently, so two schemes of concepts can fill out the same minimally interpreted proposition differently—even to the point of opposite truth-values. And just as exactly what a sketch is a sketch *of* cannot be determined except in reference to a more detailed filling in of that sketch, so what is said on a particular occasion can only be understood in reference to a particular scheme of concepts. It is in this sense that each proposition can be understood as having an index to a scheme. Yet we must be careful not to fall into a false absolutism here. For whether the proposition that grass is green is to be understood minimally, and hence as indexed to, or shared between, two conceptual schemes, or understood robustly, and hence as relative to a particular scheme, is not an absolute fact about it, but is fixed or determined itself by the overall context in which that proposition is being expressed or employed. Independent of the shifting sands of context, there is no fact of the matter.[11]

I shall put the minimal/robust distinction to further use in the next chapter. For now, note that another theoretical benefit of the distinction is that it captures the sense behind the difference many philosophers see between "ordinary" and "philosophical" concepts of *F*. Most people, including most philosophers, employ concepts all the time without any particularly strong metaphysical orientation. In the terms of the minimal/robust distinction, this is because most of us, when speaking of our "minds" ("The mind is a terrible thing to waste") or "facts" ("The fact is that you were late again"), are speaking minimally, without a care about ultimate ontology. But to explain this fact by distinguishing between "ordinary" and "philosophical" uses of "mind" is to impose an imaginary division between our philosophical activities and our other pursuits. What *is* the "ordinary" use or sense of words like "God" or "spirit" or "consciousness"? How are we to distinguish the philosophical use of these words from their use in purported "normal" circumstances? And whose sense of "ordinary" are we talking about, anyway? It is a benefit of the minimal/robust distinction that it allows us to simply drop the insistence on the difference between "ordinary" and "philosophical" senses of a word even while capturing the idea that motivated that distinction in the first place.

3.4   Concepts and Change

Family-resemblance concepts and the minimal/robust distinction illustrate how many of our concepts do not admit of fixed, determinate uses. But what is it about our practices that explains the fluidity of our concepts? And in particular, what can we say about why we pull and stretch our concepts in so many directions? These questions are questions of philosophical anthropology: they ask us to root around for the actual causes of our conceptual practices. I shall not undertake a full-fledged anthropological investigation here; nonetheless, I can make some gestures, again following Wittgenstein's lead.

Wittgenstein often compared our concepts to tools. Like a hammer, a concept is shaped as it is in order to serve a certain function—a function we need it to fill because of our interests and needs. But our needs change as our circumstances change, and we are forced to make do with the concepts we have, often clumsily. Consider trying to tighten a screw with a hammer. What would be the right way to do it? There is no right or wrong way. And yet there is a right way to use a hammer on a nail. Similarly, my concepts are often tied to a particular purpose. But if the circumstances change in radical ways, we must extend our uses of concepts to deal with the new circumstances. As in the case of the hammer, there is no fixed way to do this; we might extend a concept in any number of ways. "One might say in such a case" that the old concept has "more than one legitimate heir."[12] Hence, to talk of "the" concept of *F* can only be a remark about how we are presently employing that concept now. The demand for absolutely determinate concepts whose future use is already fixed is a demand without point in our life as lived.

To speak of the point of our concepts is to speak of the role they play in our overall worldview. In the last chapter, I noted that a worldview is an organic whole consisting not only of our conceptual scheme but also the interests we have that help explain why we have our particular concepts, the values that guide those interests, and the underlying practices and capacities that limit and define our cognitive production and intake. Of course, this linkage of our concepts and our lives is a major Wittgensteinian theme:

Concepts lead us to make investigations; [concepts] are the expression of our interest and direct our interest. (1958, sec. 570)

Further,

I want to say: an education quite different from ours might also be the foundation for quite different concepts. For here life would run on differently—What interests us would not interest them. (1987, 387–388)

I take the word "interests" here to point to our whole worldview. As Stanley Cavell says in a (justly) often-quoted passage,

[Our concepts are essentially tied to] routes of interest and feeling, senses of humor, and of significance, and of fulfillment, of what is outrageous, of what is similar to what else, what a rebuke, what forgiveness, when an utterance is an assertion, when an appeal, when an explanation—all the whirl of organism Wittgenstein calls "forms of life." (1969, 52)

As Cavell's list of examples illustrates, the point is definitely not that our concepts (and forms of life) are "conventional." We do not "invent" our concepts as one might invent a new way to file memos.

Compare a concept with a style of painting. For is even our style of painting arbitrary? Can we choose one at pleasure? (Wittgenstein 1958, 230)

Concepts, no more than styles of painting or senses of humor, cannot come and go at will. There are causes, often beyond our control, for changes in such things. This is why it would be gravely misleading to describe metaphysical pluralism in general, or relativistic Kantianism in particular, as a view according to which we construct or (deconstruct) reality. To construct something, either literally, as in the case of a house, or metaphorically, as in the case of a new law or statute, is to engage in a conscious, deliberate process of creation. The ebb and flow of our concepts more often takes place well beneath the surface of our thought.

4

The Nature of Existence

"So you are saying that human agreement decides what is true and what is false?"—It is what humans beings *say* that is true and false; and they agree in the *language* they use. That is not agreement in opinions but in forms of life.
Wittgenstein

4.1 Dilemmas Confronted

The heart of metaphysical pluralism is the paradoxical idea that there can be incompatible truths. Recently a number of critics have alleged that one can't make sense of this position without watering it down to the point of triviality. This is the danger raised by what I earlier called the *consistency dilemma* (section 1.6). Since I have clarified the notion of a conceptual scheme and examined the roots of content relativity, it is now time to confront this and other objections to pluralism.

Let's begin by looking at a particular example of metaphysical debate due to Hilary Putnam (1987, 32–33; 1992a, 120). Putnam's example has the virtue of being simple (and thus comparatively easy to discuss) but not simplistic. So while it is admittedly artificial, it serves as a good stand-in for the historically more important, but more cumbersome, examples that have motivated our interest in these types of debates (see section 1.3).

Suppose our two friends Smith and Johnson (now taken to be philosophers) are asked to look in a bag containing some marbles and count how many objects there are in the bag. Johnson looks inside and announces, "There are exactly three objects in the bag: x, y, and z." Suppose that Smith is a "mereologist," that is, a logician who believes that every part of an object is an object and that the sum of any two objects is an object. When Smith looks in the bag, she says, "There are *really* exactly seven objects in the bag: x, y, z, $x + y$, $x + z$, $y + z$, and $x + y + z$." This is a simplified version of an example ("How many objects are in my study?") that I used in chapter 1. There the example was used to illustrate why some philosophers are inclined to believe that certain metaphysical debates are irresolvable and, as a consequence, find themselves motivated to embrace some version of pluralism. The motivation stems from the fact that while both Smith's and Johnson's answers seem straightforwardly contradictory, they also seem equally correct. Putnam and the pluralist embrace both appearances: it is possible, at least, that Smith and Johnson are offering equally true, if incompatible, accounts of how many objects are in the bag. Since, on the pluralist view, there are no absolute facts about what sorts of objects exist but only facts relative to conceptual schemes, there is no such thing as "the one true answer, independent of all conceptual schemes," to the question "How many objects are there?" (Putnam, 1987, 33). Smith and Johnson are expressing propositions relative to distinct conceptual schemes.

Some readers might suspect that an absolutist could accommodate the pluralist's intuition about this particular example without abandoning her absolutism. The idea would be to adopt a kind of *ontological inclusivism*, according to which both Smith's and Johnson's answers are true, but Smith's is *more* true (or approximately true) than Johnson's. Johnson says that there are three objects in the bag; Smith argues that there are seven. The inclusivist's suggestion is that these statements needn't be conflicting if we take Johnson to be reporting only part of the truth. Of course, Smith and Johnson will *think* they are contradicting each other, in that they each take themselves (and each other) to be saying *exactly* how many objects are in the bag. But according to the ontological inclusivist, this shared belief is mistaken. While both theories are picking out different parts of the "dough" of the world, one of the schemes (Smith's) is picking out more parts than the other. Johnson's answer isn't false per se; it is only incomplete.[1]

Ontological inclusivism can seem like an attractive way to solve these cases. It is, after all, consistent with absolutism and yet does seem to satisfy our intuition that both answers are "in some sense" right. Attractive or not, however, this way of understanding ontological disputes does not work. For some ontological conflicts are not about the number of objects but about how to understand the nature of one object. Consider a debate between an Aristotelian and a Spinozist. The Aristotelian will insist that a particular person is an enduring substance with certain properties. A disciple of Spinoza, on the other hand, will claim that a person is a mode of the one substance; Nature is "personish here about," as it were. The conflict between these two theories isn't additive in the manner of the example above. Persons are either enduring, discrete particulars or modes of the one substance; they cannot be both. Given this fact, I see no reason to adopt the inclusive answer in the marble example either, but rather, prefer to take seriously Smith's and Johnson's (and Aristotle's and Spinoza's) claims to exactness where the number of objects in the bag is concerned.

Putting that objection aside, let us turn our attention to more worrisome responses to Putnam's example, in particular, the problem of how to understand the idea that there can be "incompatible but equally true" propositions, which is the question that gives rise to the consistency dilemma.

The absolutist is apt to reason as follows. Either the pluralist's incompatible but equally true accounts are logically consistent or they are not. Presumably, the pluralist's doctrine of content relativism implies that Smith's and Johnson's answers *are* logically consistent. After all, Smith's view is relative to her conceptual scheme, and Johnson's is relative to his. But then, how can they be "incompatible," as the pluralist maintains? On the contrary, it appears that they could be conjoined together in the absolutist's one true story of the world. A particularly astute critic of pluralism, Simon Blackburn notes,

The question of consistency is paramount, because it is the only reason a realist of any kind must allow to stand in the way of a concatenation of the results of different perspectives. If Putnam cannot make us see that we must allow genuinely inconsistent but "internally" true descriptions of things, then we have no reason to deny the uniqueness of truth. (1994, 19)

The sense that pluralism is a distinct philosophical position, necessarily opposed to metaphysical absolutism, begins to fade:

Of course, taken strictly, any classical philosophy can allow what Putnam says he wants: different and apparently incompatible statements can be true in the same situation because the words—in some cases, the logical words themselves—are used differently. That is, while "There are several philosophers at St. Andrews" is true in English, there are possible languages in which the same sentence is false because "there are" is used to mean something else—"there are not," for example. Nobody ever denied that, surely. (Blackburn 1994, 19)

The overall objection underlying Blackburn's comments is the consistency dilemma. According to the pluralist, propositions, including those of Smith and Johnson, are relative to conceptual schemes, and thus both answers can be "equally true." But what, asks the absolutist, does this *mean* exactly? There seem to be only two options. First, Smith and Johnson may mean something different by "there are" or "object" or "bag." If so, then Smith is simply answering an entirely different question than the question that Johnson is answering. Their answers are consistent, and therefore "equally true" (or false), but only because they are literally not talking about the same things. But this sort of equivocation over word meanings is unremarkable and entirely compatible with absolutism. On the other hand, perhaps the pluralist's idea is that Smith means by "seven" (for example) what Johnson means by "three." In this case, Smith and Johnson are expressing the same proposition in different notations. Yet this alternative is compatible with absolutism as well.

Once the pluralist concedes that Smith and Johnson's assertions are consistent, it would seem that one of these two options must capture how their respective answers are related. And either way, the absolutist is untroubled, and "pluralism" is uncontroversial.

At root, the problem concerns how content can be shared between conceptual schemes if pluralism is true.[2] Suppose that Smith and Johnson are both considering the proposition "There are three objects in the bag." According to the absolutist, the pluralist must hold that this proposition is relative to (shared by) both schemes or it is not. If it is relative to both schemes, then apparently there is absolute content after all. Perhaps, as I just suggested, Smith and Johnson have the same beliefs but express those beliefs in different notations or languages. Alternatively, perhaps matters are exactly as they appear: each philosopher is using the same conceptual scheme, speaking normal English, and considering the same (absolute) proposition. If so, then Johnson will agree that there are three objects and Smith will not. But then their answers will not be "equally true." The only other alternative is that Smith's and Johnson's schemes do *not* share content: the propositions they affirm and deny are relative to different conceptual schemes. In this case, their views can both be true, but only for the trivial reason that they are talking past one another. The upshot is that, whether or not propositions can be relative to more than one scheme, no "incompatible but equally true" propositions are possible.

As I noted in section 1.6, the consistency dilemma has an ontological face as well: the many-worlds problem. The pluralist is committed either to the existence of one world that all conceptual perspectives are perspectives of or to the existence of many worlds—one for each conceptual scheme. If the former, then the pluralist has simply admitted absolutism. If the latter, that is, if there are many worlds, then no "incompatible" conflicts can arise between Smith, Johnson, or anyone else. Blackburn notes this point as well, arguing that if the pluralist denies us the "resources to reconcile different perspectives . . . , then indeed we lose the one reality. But we also lose the notion of different perspectives, leaving ourselves with a train of ideas with no shared content, and between which no questions of compatibility or incompatibility can arise" (1994, 17).

In terms of our example, either Smith and Johnson inhabit the same world, share content, and speak the same language, or they live in different worlds, share no content, and speak different languages. Either way, absolutism would appear to triumph.

4.2   Objects and Existence

If Blackburn is right, the pluralist is wishing for something that seems inevitably beyond her reach. Specifically, what the last section has shown is that the pluralist, if she is going to have a distinct philosophical view at all, must accept each of the following propositions:

(1)   Smith and Johnson are expressing distinct propositions.

(2)   Smith and Johnson are expressing incompatible propositions.

And yet,

(3)   Smith and Johnson are expressing true propositions.

(4)   Smith and Johnson are *not* employing completely different concepts of "object" or "exist" or "number"; they are not talking past
one another.

Of course, accepting (4) is slightly redundant once one embraces (1)
through (3). If Smith and Johnson are contradicting each other, they must
be talking about the same reality.

We have our work cut out for us: how can the pluralist assert (1)
through (4) without lapsing into incoherence? The answer, I shall suggest,
lies with our concepts of object and existence. For the pluralist, these
concepts are fluid; they can be extended in radically different directions.

We can begin by looking at another recent criticism of Putnam's example by John Searle:

> But are these supposed contradictions really a problem? About [the above exam-
> ple] a realist who was a convinced conceptual relativist would say that there really
> are three objects, as the criterion for counting objects has been set in the first
> system of classification, really seven as the criterion for counting objects has been
> set in the second. And this answer removes the apparent contradictions, not by
> modifying or abandoning external realism but by simply pointing out that the
> criterion for counting objects has been set in two different ways. (1995, 163)

In saying that the criterion for counting objects has been set in two different ways, Searle would appear to agree with Blackburn: if pluralism is
reduced to claiming that words like "object" can mean different things
to different people, it is not a distinct philosophical view, because no
philosopher has ever denied that such words can have multiple meanings.[3]

In one sense, the supposition that words like "object" or "exist" mean
different things to different people is indeed quite obvious and unremarkable. There is nothing about the sound made by "object" that forces anyone to mean one thing rather than another by that word. It is possible for
"object" to mean "cat." Language, as we say, is conventional. Further, it
is quite clear that the word does have different meanings in ordinary English. Compare "That is a beautiful art object" with "The object of your
desire will forever elude you."

Yet to stop here would be to overlook an important point. Ontologists,
like our fictional friends Smith and Johnson, are not concerned with how
"object" might be used in the art or literary world. When philosophers
ask what sorts of objects exist, they are concerned with "object" in the

broadest possible sense of the word, the sense in which art objects and objects of desire are both objects. They are interested in the *minimal concept* of an object that we use when we concern ourselves with the most ultimate, basic, or fundamental objects in the universe. And this concept of an object is taken not only as the ultimate concept of an object but also as *absolute*, that is, as having a determinate use in every possible application (section 3.1). Thus, the controversial point that the pluralist is making about "object" relates only to *this* concept of an object (what we might call the "metaphysical concept of an object"). I shall argue that there neither is nor could be such a concept of an object, *where that concept is taken to be absolute and determinate*, and that the contrary assumption, besides being the root of a good deal of nonsense in philosophy, is what is at the heart of the consistency dilemma and related objections to pluralism.

First, I need to clarify a bit further the alleged concept in question. Generally speaking, analytic metaphysicians take an object to be whatever can be referred to by a singular term, or (what is essentially the same thing) as whatever can be the value of a bound variable in the propositional calculus.[4] The basic idea is that objects (or if one wishes, "things") are whatever we refer to or talk about. So if we understand the role that singular terms play in our language or if we understand quantification in elementary logic, we do apparently have a simple set of necessary and sufficient conditions for being an object: an object, in the metaphysical sense, is a possible referent of a singular term. Thus, literally, everything is an object; anything to which we refer, including numbers, propositions, battles, and mice, are all objects (if we are indeed referring, as we appear to be when speaking sentences that contain such words). To put it more precisely, if, in predicating of a singular term, I assert a true proposition, then the term in question must refer to an object.

To say that this conception of an object is a widely shared assumption in logic and analytic philosophy is to understate the case considerably.[5] Students of philosophy are nursed on it even as they make their first stumbling attempts to grasp quantification theory. So Searle is simply mistaken if he is claiming that the "criterion" for counting objects has been deliberately set differently by Smith and Johnson. If Smith and Johnson are metaphysicians, then by their own lights they will be sharing the same minimal and absolute concept of an object, *not employing different concepts*! And so it will be for most other metaphysical debates, including ones that we are inclined to think matter, e.g., debates over the existence of God, or minds, or the fundamental particles of physics. In our little metaphysical debate between Johnson and Smith, as well as in all other serious metaphysical debates, it seems wrong to say that the participants in the debate are simply equivocating over terms.

Why do philosophers think that there is a determinate metaphysical concept of an object? The root cause, it seems to me, is the intuitive connection that exists between "object" and "existence." The connection in question can be demonstrated as follows. According to standard logic, to say that x is an object that is F is just to say that there is an x that is F, or, to revert to the symbols of logic, $(\exists x)Fx$.[6] For the contemporary metaphysician, to talk of objects is simply to talk of what exists; in Quine's ringing phrase, "to be is to be the value of a bound variable."[7] Hence, the absolutist will argue, since it is clear that the concept of existence is absolutely determinate, the concept of an object must be absolute. And from this it follows that metaphysical questions as to what sorts of objects exist are subject to absolute answers.

The assumption here is that our notions of objecthood and existence are best captured by the crystalline picture of concepts, the picture that understands a concept's application conditions to be determined in all future circumstances of use. In the case of the concept of existence, this implies that there is always one and only one correct answer to the question of whether something exists (section 3.3). On the metaphysical level, it implies that everything to which the concept correctly applies shares a unique common property. Such a property would be what distinguishes existing from nonexisting objects.

But here we have a problem. According to the metaphysical concept of an object, not to mention the commonsense concept, there are no objects that do not exist. Thus, there *could* be no property that would exclude existing from nonexisting objects, since there are and could be no nonexisting objects. Therefore, the idea that there is a property that all and only existing things have in common, a property that distinguishes existence from nonexistence, is an idea with no content. Existence neither has, nor could have, an essence.

This argument rests on a fairly basic principle. If there could be no properties that individuate some alleged kind of things from other kinds, then there is no sense talking of a "kind" at all. The very idea of an object in the metaphysical sense insures that this is the case for "existing object." Hence there is no kind marked out by any application of the concept of existence. Thus existence has no nature.

To make this argument is to repeat in different words Kant's familiar point that existence is not a property. The concept of existence is that most basic of concepts. It is not a characteristic of something but is what must be presupposed for us to make sense of there being any characteristics at all. And yet this is the undoing of the metaphysical absolutist's perspective on existence. For if existence is not absolute in that there is no common property shared by all existents, then the door is open to taking "exist" as similar to "game" or "art." To do so is to take our concept of existence as a flexible concept that is learned initially by reference to certain paradigms and then extended past those paradigms as experience requires. Consider, for instance, the different paradigms being employed in the following common statements:

- There are no more cookies: you've eaten them all.
- Santa Claus does not exist.
- There are rules in this house, young man!
- Once upon a time, there was a very good prince . . .

In the first statement, the cookies have ceased to exist because they have been eaten. In the second, Santa Claus does not exist because he is fictional, or imaginary. In the third, rules exist in that one ought to do some things in the house and refrain from doing others. And in the fourth, a prince is being said to have existed, under the presupposition of a make-believe context. My point is not that there are distinct concepts of "existence" at work here, but that the one concept is being used correctly but in different paradigmatic ways, *none of which can be singled out as "the" way to use the concept of existence.* To exist is not to do anything, to be anything, to share anything special or unique with anything else; our concept of existence is learned by extrapolating from examples such as the ones above. And if our concept of existence is not an absolute concept, then (because of the intrinsic connection between the two) neither is the metaphysical concept of an object. For the pluralist, basic concepts (of which the concept of existence is surely a paradigm) are not unbending but fluid. Like "game," our concepts of "object" and "existence" are flexible concepts, subject to radical extensions of use.[8]

The point I've been suggesting, namely the fluidity of existence and objecthood, has been made by Putnam. As he says in responding to the example I've been discussing involving the number of objects in a room (an example Putnam himself introduced into the literature, recall),

As a layman might well put it, "It depends on what you mean by object." But the consequence is startling; the very meaning of existential quantification is left indeterminate as long as the notion of an "object in the logical sense" is left unspecified. So it looks as if *the logical connectives themselves have a variety of possible uses.* (1989, 112)

When I discuss this passage with philosophers, I find that many of them interpret Putnam as claiming that the words "object," "existence," and the existential quantifier are ambiguous. This seems to me incorrect as an interpretation of what Putnam is trying to say, although I concede that the matter is perhaps unclear (partly because the word "ambiguous" is ambiguous). In any event, I need to stress immediately that, according to my own view, the pluralist's denial that the concept of existence is absolute should not be confused with the claim that the word "existence" is equivocal or semantically ambiguous. Insofar as it makes sense to talk about the univocality or equivocality of words (which it surely does, in many contexts), the English word "existence" is quite univocal. Unlike words such as "bank," "rise," or "beat," English speakers do not take "exist" or "there is" to commonly express more than one concept or meaning. Intuitively, to deny that there is life on Mars or to claim that there is a God is to use the same concept. Such intuitions are further bolstered by the point often attributed to Frege, that our concepts of number and existence are closely related. I can deny that there are any witches by saying that the number of witches is 0, and I can affirm that there are electrons by saying that the number of electrons is greater than 1. Since we take it that we mean the same thing by "3" when we say there are 3 apples, 3 oranges, and 3 main causes for teenage smoking, it follows that "existence" too is univocal.

Of course, as we saw in the last chapter, "game" is also univocal; Checkers, baseball, and bouncing a ball up against the garage are all games, and yet there is no one property that they all share in common. And yet our concept of game is not absolute; it is a flexible concept par excellence; its use is not determinate. Thus a word like "game" can be used univocally without being used absolutely. And this will be how the pluralist looks at existence as well.

J. L. Austin made a similar point about "real." He noted first that while "real" is in one sense a perfectly normal word, in that it has a firmly established use in ordinary language, it also

is not a normal word at all, but highly exceptional; exceptional in this respect that, unlike "yellow" or "horse" or "walk," it does not have one single, specifiable, always-the-same meaning. (Even Aristotle saw through this idea.) Nor does it have a large number of different meanings—it is not ambiguous, even "systematically." (1962, 64)

Austin's point, as he goes on to make clear, is that there is no characteristic common to all things that are or could be called "real." The concept expressed by "real" is what Wittgenstein would have called a "family resemblance" concept. According to Austin, this fact that there is no unique property shared by all things real is due to the function that the word or concept has in our language. In the case of "real," he says, it is the negative use that "wears the trousers" or is the most basic (1962, 70). Simply put, we typically say that something is "real" when we wish to exclude ways in which that something may *not* be real. In saying that I saw a real duck in the pond, I am saying that it was, e.g., not a fake duck, it was not a decoy. But since the ways in which something may *not* be real are multitudinous, it follows that the ways in which something *can be* real are similarly wide and varied. There is no common property shared by all things real.

The concept of existence *sometimes* functions in the same way as "real." Consider a child's insistence, in the face of another child's taunting, that Santa *does* exist. The point of the claim is that Santa Claus is *not imaginary*. But such an explanation does not hold across the board. For in saying, "There is beer in the fridge," I *may* be trying to exclude cases where there is no beer, but I can also be simply informing you of a relevant fact. The fact that our use of "real" and "exist" diverge in this way is not surprising, for that which exists may not be real, but everything that is real exists. Yet the two concepts do share this similarity: neither is absolute, or determinate, in use.

Of course, there are objections that can be made against the conception of existence I've been discussing. To begin with, one might try arguing that there *is* a property shared by all and only existents. For instance, one might point out that the property of self-identity is shared by all existing things.[9] That is, everything is necessarily identical with itself. Could not this be the essence of existence? If so, then the concepts of existence and objecthood would be shown to be absolute after all.

In reply, several points seem relevant. To begin with, to take the property of self-identity as the defining essence of existence seems to commit one to the view that existence itself is a property, which is false. Of course, it might be objected that the original point was meant as a conceptual claim only: the idea is that "*x* exists" and "*x* is identical with itself" are somehow conceptually connected. This is also implausible, however. First, to say that something is self-identical is not to say that it exists, if only because one can suppose that a person might not exist without supposing (incoherently) that he might not be self-identical. Second, from the fact that every thing is identical to itself, it follows that Santa Claus is identical to Santa Claus, but it is certainly not a *conceptual* consequence of "Santa Claus = Santa Claus" that Santa Claus exists.

Another line of objection might favor a more direct attempt to show that the metaphysical concept of an object is absolute even if the related concept of existence is not. After all, we have already seen above that contemporary logicians and metaphysicians take objects to be what can be referred to by singular terms (or what can be the value of bound variables). Is this not a precise and absolute definition of "object"? Only if "being able to be referred to by a singular term" denotes a property, which it does not.

Whether I or anyone can doubt, believe, or imagine that something is the case is a fact concerned with the person in question. Facts about what a person believes are therefore not fit for divining identities between other objects, since one person may believe something to fall under a certain description and another may not believe it without the something in question changing its properties in any way whatsoever. The same goes with the alleged properties "being able to be referred to by a singular term" or "being able to be the value of a bound variable." Referring—like believing, knowing, imagining, doubting, and recognizing—is a *human ac-*

tivity, and hence statements about what can or cannot be referred to are statements about *us,* that is, about the humans doing the referring, believing, or knowing. To say that objects are whatever can be referred to by singular terms is no more informative than saying that thoughts are those things we cannot doubt we have. In both cases, we have failed to pick out any genuine property to ascribe to what we are attempting to define. In the latter case, as well as the former case, we have managed to say something true, certainly, but it is a truth that tells us nothing about the nature, the essence, of thought or object.

While some will find this reply satisfactory (perhaps even obvious), many will object to its controversial premise that reference is a human activity, rather than, e.g., an objective causal relationship between words and things.[10] Thus, let me add the following point, which I think suffices by itself to answer the objection. To say that objects are essentially whatever can be referred to by singular terms is uninformative for the same reason that any attempt to define the essence of existence is bound to be uninformative. For such a definition, in order to have content, must distinguish between what can be referred to by singular terms (or can be the value of a bound variable) and what cannot be, with objects being said to fall in the former category. The problem is that we cannot formulate such a distinction without violating the definition in question, for if all and only objects are what can be referred to by singular terms, then literally every *thing* must be such, and hence there cannot be a distinction between *what* can be referred to by singular terms and *what* cannot be. And thus the proposed absolutist definition is without content.

At this juncture, I wish to emphasize that in criticizing the "absolute concept of an object," I am *not* attacking Quine's infamous "criterion of ontological commitment." According to Quine, "we are convicted of a particular ontological presupposition if, and only if, the alleged presuppositum has to be reckoned among the entities over which our variables range in order to render one of our affirmations true" (1953, 13). Taken for what it is—as simply a useful standard for deciding what objects your theories commit you to, a technique in other words—Quine's criterion is unobjectionable. In the same way, the minimal concept of an object itself is not necessarily the target of the pluralist. The target of the pluralist's criticism is the *absolutist interpretation* or construal of these ideas.

More specifically, there is no theoretical reason that a metaphysical pluralist can't use Quine's criterion—can't believe that objects are whatever
are the values of our bound variables—as long as she does not claim that
the concept is absolute and determinate.

As a matter of fact, however, the "Quinean" conception of an object
is generally taken to be an absolute notion by those who employ it. The
usefulness of such notions is very much tied, in fact, to the most prevalent
absolutist metaphysic: global materialism. To see this, notice that on the
surface, taking an object to be whatever can be referred to by a singular
term (or whatever is the value of a bound variable) seemingly commits
one to the existence of many *nonphysical* objects. For example, "The
Battle of Shiloh was one of the bloodiest of the American Civil War"
implies that there is such an object as the Battle of Shiloh. "The number
of planets in the solar system is nine" implies that there is such a thing
as the number 9. "Sherlock Holmes was smarter than Watson" implies
that there is something referred to by "Sherlock Holmes." None of these
objects fit easily into a materialist or physical conceptual scheme. Of
course, the contemporary metaphysician will hastily remind us that by
employing the technique of "paraphrase" (as it is called) one can illustrate
that in many cases of ordinary speech, what appears to be a reference to
an object is really not. A canonical example of this are assertions such
as "The grin on Smith's face is broad." Surely, it is said, those who utter
statements such as this do not mean to imply that there (really) are grins,
and common sense can be protected by simply noting that such a statement can be paraphrased as "Smith grinned broadly," which implies the
existence of no object other than Smith. Thus we find that contemporary
materialist metaphysicians are continuously busy with the "paraphrase
project"—or the business of paraphrasing statements that appear to de-
note suspicious-sounding objects of one sort or another into more ontologically innocent statements, that is, statements that refer only to
physical objects.

Of course, as a number of commentators have pointed out, paraphrase
is symmetrical.[11] If "The grin on Smith's face is broad" can be paraphrased by "Smith grins broadly," then the reverse must hold as well,
simply in virtue of what is meant by "paraphrase." Thus it is difficult to
understand why we should take the former statement to be any more or

less "object denoting" than the latter. The metaphysician will reply, with Peter van Inwagen (1993, 347), that by paraphrasing the first statement into the second, he has shown that the appearance that the first statement refers to grins is just that, "an appearance," and not reality. But of course, one could just as well say that it is the latter sentence that is deceptive, that "Smith grins broadly" only appears *not* to refer to a grin when in fact it does. Independently of a prior commitment to metaphysical absolutism, it seems that paraphrase is of dubious worth in relieving us from treating grins, sakes, and the like as full-fledged objects.

A philosopher convinced of metaphysical pluralism, however, is not apt to engage in the paraphrase project. Insofar as it is not simply an amusing parlor game, philosophical paraphrase only makes sense against the background of metaphysical absolutism. If one assumes a global and absolute materialist ontology for the universe, any references to what look like nonphysical entities (numbers, grins, and fictional characters, for instance) will automatically be suspect and in need of being "paraphrased away." But the pluralist needn't make such assumptions. For the pluralist, materialism is only one metaphysical scheme among others. We may have compelling pragmatic or explanatory reasons to employ the materialist framework, but no such framework can be the absolute truth. So it is not Quine's actual criterion for ontological commitment that is wrong, but rather the assumption of absolutism motivating the paraphrase projects so closely linked to Quine's criterion.

4.3 Dilemmas Resolved

I have argued that the metaphysician's minimal concept of an object, according to which an object is whatever exists, is a fluid concept. Like other minimal concepts we have examined (section 3.3), it is fluid in that it can be extended in two different appropriate but incompatible directions. To the objection that our minimal concept of an object is defined by the concept of existence, I have argued that the concept of existence is itself flexible, like the concept of a game. To take the concept of existence in this way is to admit that because of the availability of more than one legitimate paradigm, it is possible to be confronted with two inconsistent but equally legitimate applications of that concept. The implication of both points is that one can reach different but equally true answers to questions about objects and existence without employing different concepts.

Let us return to our example. As you recall, Smith and Johnson were having an ontological debate over the amount of objects in a particular bag. According to Johnson, there are three, according to Smith, seven. We saw that the pluralist needs to be able to affirm the following four propositions.

(1)   Smith and Johnson are expressing distinct propositions.

(2)   Smith and Johnson are expressing incompatible propositions.

(3)   Smith and Johnson are expressing true propositions.

(4)   Smith and Johnson are *not* employing completely different concepts of "object" or "exist" or "number"; they are not talking past one another.

We are now in a position to explain how this circumstance is possible, and therefore to answer the objections. First, since "exactly three" implies "not exactly seven," and vice versa, in an obvious sense of "distinct proposition," Smith and Johnson are expressing distinct propositions. So (1) is satisfied. Smith and Johnson are also employing the same notion of existence or objecthood (and will, of course, take themselves to be doing so) even while they are extending those concepts from a basis of different paradigms. So (4) is satisfied. Johnson, for instance, takes paradigm objects to be the "middle-sized dry goods" of daily life. So when he looks in the bag and sees three marbles, he infers that there are three and only three objects in the bag. Smith, on the other hand, is impressed with the fact that one can discuss and assign properties to parts and wholes, and hence finds it natural to take the number of objects in the bag to be seven. Finally, just as it can be true that *x* is a game in relation to one paradigm example of a game and false relative to another paradigm without this fact causing so much as a whisper of cognitive dissonance, so too is the same move completely acceptable with "exist" or "object." So (3) is satisfied as well.

This leaves (2). Suppose that Johnson says that there are three objects in the bag and Smith denies it. In what sense of "incompatible" are

Smith's and Johnson's assertions incompatible? According to the pluralist, they are (or could be) extending their shared minimal concept of an object differently. Thus the propositions they are expressing are relative to different conceptual schemes and are therefore logically consistent. At the same time, there is a clear and important sense in which the pair of propositions *are* incompatible: *if these propositions were relative to the same scheme, they would be inconsistent.* This fact is necessarily true of that pair of propositions: in every possible world where these propositions are relative to the same scheme, only one is true. And it is in precisely this sense that Johnson and Smith are rightly said to be expressing consistent but incompatible propositions.

Some might worry about whether we can make sense of this "counterfactual" analysis of incompatibility. In general, of course, we take all sorts of analogous counterfactual propositions to be true: "If we hadn't met, I would be dreadfully unhappy," we say, or again, "If I were born in the tenth century, I would not live very long." Without question, there are complicated technical issues concerning how to understand the logic of such statements, but these issues are not the special concern of just the pluralist.

A more relevant worry would be that the pluralist's own doctrine of content relativism prohibits the use of such an analysis, since any claim about what *would* be the case if some proposition *were* not relative to a particular scheme might appear to assume that it makes sense to talk about propositions independently of schemes. Content relativity demands that a proposition is determinate only within a particular conceptual scheme. How, then, can we consider a proposition independently of that scheme? We seem to have lost our idea of what the proposition is exactly.

At root, the worry here goes back to the problem of shared content (see section 4.1). The assumption being made is that propositions cannot be relative to more than one scheme. If they are relative to more than one scheme, the absolutist will claim that there is absolute content after all. On the other hand, if a proposition can be relative only to a particular scheme, then it is hard to make sense of what would be the case with regard to that proposition were it relative to some *other* scheme.

There are two grave problems with this reasoning, however. First, it incorrectly assumes that a shared proposition (one relative to more than one scheme) is an absolute proposition. This is false. To say that the truth conditions of a proposition are relative to more than one scheme is not to say that these conditions are independent of all schemes. More important, the assumption that "either a proposition is relative to more than one scheme, or it is not" is also false on the pluralist's view. As I argued in section 3.3, there are no absolute answers to such questions. Just as there is no such thing as "the" concept of an object, so there is no such thing as "the" proposition that there are three objects in the bag. Questions about how to count propositions (do we have one proposition relative to two schemes or two distinct propositions each relative to a different scheme?) are themselves not absolute but relative to context. Specifically, one can consider such concepts and propositions minimally or robustly. Minimally speaking, the same proposition can be considered relative to more than one scheme. Robustly speaking, it cannot.[12]

Therefore, it makes sense to ask whether some pair of propositions would be consistent *if they were relative to the same scheme*, because in so doing, we are drawing upon the fact that these propositions, robustly interpreted, share some minimal content. We are asking what would be the case if the minimal content of both propositions were extended along similar lines relative to the same scheme. Minimally speaking, Smith's and Johnson's assertions agree in scheme but not in truth.

What about the ontological face of the consistency dilemma—what I called in section 1.6 the many-worlds problem? For there to be incompatible propositions between different schemes, the propositions in question must be *about the same world*—referring to the same object or objects. But how is this possible if facts and objects are relative to conceptual schemes?

Pluralists have gone different ways on this issue. Nelson Goodman, for instance, takes the radical view of treating conceptual schemes (what he calls "versions") as true of radically distinct worlds:

A true version is true in some worlds, a false version in none. Thus the multiple worlds of conflicting true versions are actual worlds, not the merely possible worlds or nonworlds of false versions. (1984, 31)

For Goodman, there is no "problem of many worlds," because it is simply a fact that there are many worlds—one for each conceptual scheme or "version."

There are at least two reasons to avoid Goodman's suggestion. First, absolutism is true *within* each of Goodman's worlds. Each individual world has a story true of it. So we've saved pluralism in one sense only by admitting absolutism in another. Second, the idea that there is literally more than one world—that you and I, for instance, might literally, as opposed to metaphorically, live in separate universes—is anti-intuitive in the extreme. Minimally speaking, our concept of reality, or "world," implies that said reality impinges on all of us; there is one world we share. An underlying presupposition of our actual lives is that we all participate in a reality larger than ourselves. Of course, Goodman might reply that he is rejecting that conception of reality and giving us another. But then I cannot accept his conception on normative grounds, for it ends up alienating people from one another. If we live in different worlds, why should I care what happens to yours? Why should I have a concern for a world that I can never inhabit? The hypothesis that there are many worlds would seem to imply a radical separateness between people that I find objectionable.

Fortunately, there is another solution. The answer here is much the same as it was above in the case of the consistency dilemma. Understood minimally, Smith's and Johnson's assertions *are* about the same sort of objects. The conditions under which they successfully refer to such objects will be the same. Of course, interpreted robustly, they are talking about different sorts of objects, but even then their assertions are incompatible in the subjunctive sense explained above: were the respective propositions relative to the same scheme, they would be inconsistent. This should not make us think that they are inhabiting different *worlds*. For they obviously do share a world, *a minimal world*. Given their different conceptual categories, *this one world* can present itself to them in radically distinct and incompatible ways. It follows that our concepts of "world" or "reality" are fluid in the same manner as our concepts of object and existence. Just as we can apply a shared but fluid concept of an object in radically distinct ways without taking ourselves to have switched concepts, so we can see Smith and Johnson as implicitly extending their shared notion of reality.

The matter is complicated in that we are now assuming a standpoint that "overlooks" or encompasses both Smith's and Johnson's viewpoints.

This allows us to see that Smith and Johnson are sharing schemes that interpret their shared reality differently. Such an "overlook" may not be available to us in all cases, of course. There may be some cases where we will be unable (either practically, morally, or physically) to occupy an independent standpoint that encompasses the two other conflicting schemes. But even if we cannot grasp how two schemes are representing the same world, it is consistent with pluralism to hold (as our concept of a single world implies) that such a standpoint is always possible in the abstract sense.

We shall return to this notion of a shared reality—of THE WORLD, as Putnam sometimes says—in the last chapter. I shall conclude this section with two remaining comments. First, because of the centrality of existence and objecthood to metaphysics, a pluralist account of these concepts has sweeping implications for a considerable amount of other concepts. Among the most obvious ones to be affected are the concepts of number, identity, reference, property, substance, and, as Putnam has noted, the logical connectives themselves. Clearly, a fully worked-out pluralism would include an account of the fluidity of these concepts as well. That such accounts can be given is, I hope, indicated by the discussion above of the flexible nature of existence. In any event, the pluralist strategy will remain the same in each of the various examples I surveyed in chapter 1. The idea is to show that the central metaphysical concepts in each case are fluid, by being either family-resemblance concepts or minimal concepts subject to divergent extensions.

Second, I need to stress that the pluralist can evade the consistency dilemma, as articulated by Blackburn and others, just so long as she *can* affirm (1) through (4). She need not do so in any particular case. That is, for it not to be necessarily true that there is one and only one answer to questions about what ultimately exists in the universe, it need only be *possible* that there be more than one true answer. To put it in terms of a distinction made in section 2.4, a *weak modal pluralism* remains inconsistent with metaphysical absolutism. Thus a pluralist is not committed to embracing every answer to questions about what exist. Not every answer need be as true as every other in order for it be false that there must be one true story of the world.

4.4   The Idealism Objection

There still remains one objection to the coherency of pluralism that I need to address. That objection is that metaphysical pluralism is just a form of idealism in disguise. Idealism, classically understood, is the view that ultimate reality is entirely mental. Hence classical idealism (and here I think of Berkeley and Bradley) is best understood as a form of absolutism: it holds that there is one true way the world is, namely a mental way. So it would be a mistake to identify pluralism with classical idealism; pluralism is just as opposed to an absolutist idealism as it is to an absolutist "realism."

Of course, this point doesn't answer the question of whether pluralism might still be some other form of idealism. In particular, the doctrine of content relativity would seem to imply that all of reality depends on the mind in some way. If so, then pluralism could justifiably be labeled as a form of idealism. The reasoning behind this suspicion is easy to see. I have said that pluralism involves the relativity of facts to conceptual schemes, and I have said that I take facts to be equivalent to obtaining states of affairs. Furthermore, I have said that conceptual schemes are schemes of concepts. Hence it may seem that according to the pluralist, if there are no minds, then there are no concepts; if there are no concepts, there are no conceptual schemes; and if there are no conceptual schemes, then presumably there are no facts. In particular, if there were no minds, the earth would not be spherical, nor rotate around the sun, nor occupy an orbit between that of Venus and Mars. And surely this is absurd.

The pluralist needn't accept this conclusion. Pluralism is not the view that "everything is just a matter of words" or that "everything depends on our thought." It is true that the pluralist believes that we can say nothing outside of a conceptual scheme, and therefore that all facts are relative to conceptual schemes. But this does not require the pluralist to also deny that the world, reality, contributes to, or places constraints on everything we say. Nor does it mean that just any old statement can be true. What pluralism does imply is that one can't describe the world's constraints on us from an absolute standpoint. Even the constraints admit, in principle, of more than one true description.

The idea is that within a certain conceptual scheme, the facts are what they are independent of any of our particular beliefs. Within my scheme, the influence of gravity on physical bodies is simply a fact, and there is nothing I can do about it. "In any sense of 'independent' that I can understand," as Putnam says, whether gravity influences physical bodies "is independent of the way we talk" (1992b, 433). For within our conceptual scheme, it is certainly the case that gravity would exist even if we never learned to use words; the fact that gravity influences physical bodies is thus causally independent of our beliefs or manners of speaking. And it is logically independent as well; no description of any human activity whatsoever will entail that there are gravitational effects on bodies (Putnam 1992b, 433). But this does not mean that the facts about gravity are nonrelative. Gravity's effects on us and other bodies do not depend on my beliefs or the beliefs of any human beings, but the facts about gravity are still relative to a particular (in our case, human) conceptual scheme.

It is crucial to see that the pluralist extends this relativity to modal and counterfactual facts as well. Consider a possible world where humans don't exist. We would agree, of course, that our absence in this world has no effect at all on whether there are stars in that world. But our agreement about what could or could not exist without humans around is made in the actual world, and hence *within a conceptual scheme*. What we suppose would or could be the case independently of conceptual schemes is itself relative to a conceptual scheme (compare Sosa 1993a, 623–624). So the pluralist is not embarrassed by intuitions to the effect that the stars do not depend for their existence on our concepts. It is consistent with pluralism to acknowledge that, relative to one's own conceptual scheme, there would still be stars without conceptual schemes. Yet this modal fact is as relative as any other metaphysical fact.

These answers are not apt to change the minds of many absolutist critics. This does not mean that they are bad answers, but it does reveal the air of intractability that surrounds such debates. At what we might call the "object" level, the pluralist insists that she can assert all the facts, agree to all the same truths, that the absolutist can. The pluralist and the absolutist will both say that the sky would still be blue even if all of us dropped dead tomorrow. But at the "meta" level, there is a disagreement.

The pluralist points out that what propositions are true at the object level are true only relative to a conceptual scheme. The absolutist not only denies this; he believes that if the pluralist were right (at the meta level), then some propositions that we would like to think are true at the object level would be false. For instance, according to the absolutist, if the pluralist were right, if there were no conceptual schemes, there would be no stars. But, of course, this is the case only on the assumption that the pluralist is in fact *wrong*. The absolutist is assuming that the proposition that there would be stars without conceptual schemes can only be nonrelatively true. But this is just what the pluralist denies.

5

The Currents of Truth

All things flow.
Heraclitus

5.1   What Is Realism about Truth?

The main thesis of this book is that metaphysical pluralism is compatible with realism about truth. Minimally speaking, a proposition is true in the realist sense when things are as that proposition says they are. Some aspect of objective reality must simply be a certain way. If it is, then the proposition is true; if not, the proposition is false. The truth of the proposition hinges on the world alone, not on our thought about the world. In short, realism about truth minimally implies two commitments: (a) truth is an authentic property that some propositions have and others lack, and (b) the concept of truth is, in Putnam's words, "radically non-epistemic"; that is, whether a proposition is true (in most cases) does not depend on what I or anyone else believes or knows (Putnam 1978, 125).

While there are several different types of theories that could qualify under this definition as realist theories of truth, the most well-known realist view is certainly the *correspondence theory of truth*, or the view that a proposition is true just when it corresponds to the facts. This is often said to be what Aristotle was after when he noted, "To say that that which is *is not* or that which is not *is*, is a falsehood; and to say that that which is *is* and that which is not *is not*, is true."[1]

Given our definition of realism about truth, it follows that there are two basic ways to be an *antirealist* about the notion. First, one might deny that truth is a real feature of propositions, beliefs, statements, or the like. Views that do so are called *deflationary* accounts because they "deflate" the concept of truth to some other role than picking out a real feature of the world. Second, one might hold that the truth of a proposition consists not—as the correspondence theory holds—in its relation to something "in the world," but in its having a certain epistemic status within our experience or conceptual scheme. Truth is defined in terms of what we might call our epistemic point of view: for a proposition or belief to be true is for it to be known, justified, or warranted in some sense. Call this second type of antirealism about truth the *epistemic* account of the concept.

Prior to discussing the correspondence theory and its relation to metaphysical pluralism, I need to spend some time discussing the two broad types of antirealism about truth. In particular, we need to examine several questions that naturally arise at this point in the discussion. The first concerns the fact that metaphysical pluralism is typically assumed in the literature to imply one or another form of antirealism; we need to examine some of the reasons for this assumption and, more generally, address the question of what is to be gained by a metaphysical pluralism that is *not* antirealist. I shall argue that metaphysical pluralism does not require a deflationary or an epistemic view of truth and, further, that in view of the grave objections that face views of these sorts, the pluralist is better off not adopting them.

5.2   Antirealism about Truth: Epistemic Theories

Epistemic views of truth have a long and distinguished history, having been advocated by such philosophical luminaries as F. H. Bradley, Brand Blanshard, Charles Peirce, and William James. In more recent times, the chief champion of the epistemic theory of truth has been Hilary Putnam. Because of Putnam's importance as a pluralist, there is a clear rhetorical advantage in demonstrating that his views on truth can be pried apart from pluralism.

The canonical presentation of Putnam's epistemic conception of truth appears in his book *Reason, Truth, and History* (1981).[2] In that book, Putnam argues against what he calls metaphysical realism, which he takes to be committed by definition to the correspondence view of truth, and he advocates instead a position he calls *internal realism*:

"Truth," in an internalist view, is some sort of (idealized) rational acceptability— some sort of ideal coherence of our beliefs with each other and with our experiences as those experiences are themselves represented in our belief system—and not correspondence with mind-independent or discourse-independent "states of affairs." (1981, 49–50)

Or again:

Truth is an idealization of rational acceptability. We speak as if there were such things as epistemically ideal conditions, and we call a statement "true" if it would be justified under such conditions." (1981, 55)

In subsequent writings (1989), Putnam has denied that he was offering a "reductive" account of truth—one that explains truth in terms of "more basic" epistemic notions. Instead, he claims that the two concepts are "interdependent" (1989, 115). This remark requires some interpretation. One suggestion would be to take Putnam as advocating the following *weak conceptual equivalence*:

PT   *It is true that p if, and only if, the proposition that p would be justified in ideal epistemic conditions.*

By calling PT (Putnam's theory) a weak conceptual equivalence, we take it that PT is not providing a synonym for "true" but connecting truth to other concepts. That is, the two sides of PT have the same truth value in every possible world in virtue of their respective concepts, but they are not synonymous. Truth is "necessarily coextensive" with idealized justification.

Two questions immediately spring to mind when first encountering a theory like PT. The first is, what is meant by "ideal epistemic conditions"? The second: what theory of the nature of justification, if any, is being assumed here? As to the first question, following Alston (1996, 194) and Schmitt (1995, 113), we can roughly say that ideal epistemic conditions would be conditions where all relevant evidence is available. Epistemically speaking, circumstances are ideal with respect to a certain proposition when all reasons and data (sensory or otherwise) pertaining to the epistemic status of that proposition are readily available for consideration. To be in epistemically ideal conditions is to have all the relevant evidence at one's fingertips.[3] The second question, concerning what is meant by "justification" in this context, is a bit more tricky. There are obvious reasons for the epistemic theorist to remain neutral on this question. Debates over the nature of epistemic justification are fraught with complexity, and it would certainly be beneficial from a rhetorical standpoint, at the very least, for the advocate of PT not to have to come down on one side or the other. Nonetheless, as the first quote above indicates, Putnam himself seems inclined toward a coherence theory of epistemic justification.[4] For this reason, when Putnam talks of a belief being "ideally justified," it seems worthwhile to interpret him as meaning something like (as he says) ideal coherence. Presumably, to say that a belief is ideally coherent means that were epistemic conditions ideal, the belief would be a member of a maximally coherent system of beliefs. In what follows, I will assume that Putnam's version of PT involves a coherence theory of justification. But I do not think that PT *requires* the coherence theory, and any point I make concerning PT interpreted as involving a commitment to the coherence view of justification could be made about a version of PT that did not have that commitment.

PT shouldn't be confused with a simpler epistemic conception of truth, according to which truth is identified with justification or warrant simpliciter. Simple epistemic theories of truth have obvious problems, as Putnam notes (1981, 55). There are clearly some beliefs that are now true but unjustified, and others that are justified but not true. As for the former sort, there are many true empirical propositions, about rocks on the surface of Mars, for instance, that are not presently justified but may well be justified in the future. Of course, since we believe only what we take ourselves to be justified in believing, examples of the other sort—propositions that are now justified but false—are difficult to cite, but few of us would deny that our past experience has proven that we have been mistaken about which of our beliefs are true. To put it another way, truth is stable and unchanging, while the epistemic status of a belief (i.e., whether it is justified or unjustified) may change positively or negatively as new information comes in. Putnam's point in talking of idealized justification—what would be justified when *all* the relevant information is at hand—is that idealized justification meets the stability constraint. And yet PT remains entirely epistemic; there is nothing about the world "making" or "causing" propositions to be true mentioned in PT. According to PT, a proposition's truth consists only in its being the case that it would be justified were epistemic conditions ideal. This is still antirealism about truth.

Why would a metaphysical pluralism of the sort I've discussed seem so compatible with a theory of truth along the lines of PT? There seem to be two main reasons. The first reason is that a theory like PT appears to allow for incompatible truths in a very straightforward sense—the very heart of pluralism. Here is Putnam on the matter:

> Why should there not sometimes be equally coherent but incompatible conceptual schemes which fit our experiential beliefs equally well? If truth is not (unique) correspondence then the possibility of a certain pluralism is opened up. (1981, 73)

The thought here would seem to be this: if truth is idealized justification and "justification" here means "coherence," then two distinct and even inconsistent, but equally coherent, sets of beliefs are certainly possible. In fact, the beliefs of Johnson and Smith with regard to the objects in the bag seem like ideal candidates. So, adopting PT, according to Putnam, would allow for propositions that are incompatible but equally true (that is, equally coherent in ideal epistemic conditions), in other words, propositions of the sort embraced by metaphysical pluralism. Indeed, whatever your theory of justification, it seems that two incompatible propositions or beliefs can be equally *justified*. For example, given our relative states of information, you and I might be entirely justified in our contrary opinions about the movement of the ball on the court during a basketball game. And even in the ideal epistemic state, when all relevant information has been collected, we can imagine equally coherent but distinct sets of beliefs—belief sets whose components are equally evidentially supported by one another. So PT and metaphysical pluralism seem compatible.

Of course, the fact that pluralism is compatible with PT is no concern for someone like myself, who believes that pluralism is *also* compatible with a realist view of truth. More problematic for my view is the contention that PT and metaphysical pluralism are compatible because there is a *stronger connection* of some sort between them. It might appear, in other words, that a prior commitment to metaphysical pluralism *entails a theory of truth like PT*, whether or not PT entails pluralism.

It is not entirely clear why this entailment should seem plausible. One suggestion is that a Quinean model of conceptual schemes may encourage an epistemic view of truth. As I noted in section 2.3, Putnam often seems of two minds about conceptual schemes. Sometimes he seems to embrace a Quinean view; at other times he seems drawn toward something more like the Wittgensteinian model I advocated earlier. An assumption of the Quinean view, for instance, can be seen lurking in the background in a passage from Putnam that we've already discussed. The passage I have in mind includes Putnam's rhetorical question "Why should there not sometimes be equally coherent but incompatible conceptual schemes which fit our experiential beliefs equally well?" Putnam is here implicitly assuming that conceptual schemes can be coherent, and hence that two schemes might be "equally" coherent. Within epistemology, coherence theorists of justification claim that it is beliefs (and derivatively, the propositions that make up the content of those beliefs) that have or lack the property of coherence. This is as it should be; after all, epistemology is concerned with what we should *believe*. Hence, a typical coherence theorist claims that an individual belief or proposition is justified insofar as it is a member of a coherent set of beliefs (or propositions). According to the Quinean model of conceptual schemes I discussed in chapter 2, "our conceptual scheme" just is our set or beliefs, or as Quine might say, the set of sentences we accept. So when Putnam asks, "Why can't there be equally coherent conceptual schemes?" he would seem to be thinking of conceptual schemes as sets of beliefs, propositions, or sentences—one of the defining elements of the Quinean model of a conceptual scheme.

Whether or not my analysis of Putnam's thinking here is correct, once one *does* adopt the Quinean vision of conceptual schemes, then if one isn't drawn to deflationism, a theory like PT would seem the natural option. The pluralist slogan is "Propositions are relative to conceptual schemes." In particular, the proposition that grass is green is relative to a scheme. But if schemes are understood as sets of beliefs or propositions, then the most natural way to interpret content relativity would understand that a proposition is "relative to a scheme" just when it is included on the list of propositions/beliefs that make up the scheme. Of course, not all propositions that are presently part of our scheme are true. Hence a proposition is true, on this way of thinking, when it is ideally justified— "ideally coherent" as Putnam says. In other words, a true proposition is one that would be included at the hypothetical point when we give a complete and maximally coherent description of the world from the point of view of the conceptual scheme in question. Once we start thinking that relativity to a scheme means "being included on the list of propositions that make up the scheme," then it is likely that we will also think that being true for a scheme will consist in being included on that list as it will be at the ideal epistemic limit.

So a Quinean model of conceptual schemes suggests an epistemic view of truth, and perhaps this fact explains the widespread assumption that pluralism involves a commitment to a theory like PT. But as I argued in chapter 2, the Quinean model is not ultimately defensible. Furthermore, the metaphysical pluralist is not roped to the Quinean picture. There is another, better theory of conceptual schemes available to the pluralist, one that avoids the problems associated with the Quinean view—including, as we now see, the problem of being tied to an epistemic theory of truth. Once the assumption of the Quinean model is cast aside, there is no reason to think that adopting metaphysical pluralism requires one to adopt an epistemic theory of truth.

So far, then, we have seen that there is no reason that a metaphysical pluralist *must* embrace an epistemic account of truth along the lines of PT. This is a good thing, for PT and related views face numerous troubling objections. Since the primary focus of this work is not to prove that one theory of truth is superior to the others, I do not intend to drag the reader through an exhaustive critical survey of the weaknesses of epistemic theories like Putnam's. Nonetheless, there is a certain value in briefly cataloguing a few of the more important objections that have been made against PT, if only to motivate the reader to take seriously the account of truth that will be discussed later in the chapter.

Perhaps the most straightforward objection to PT has been made by William Alston (1996, 199 ff). According to Alston, it is entirely conceivable that there are propositions that are true but not justifiable even in ideal epistemic conditions:

Might there not be states of affairs, or even entire realms or aspects of reality, that are totally inaccessible to human cognition? If so, propositions to the effect that such states of affairs obtain will be true, even though no beliefs or statements bearing those propositions as their content would be justifiable in an epistemically ideal situation. (1996, 200)

Alston's contention that there could be such states of affairs seems entirely reasonable. Human cognition is surely limited in some respects, and it seems entirely possible that there are aspects of reality that our limited minds are incapable of grasping. Plausibly, for instance, there is a fact of the matter about what it is like to be bat—there are certain propositions, that is, that are true concerning the inner life of a creature with sonar. If Thomas Nagel (1974) is correct, no amount of physical evidence would even justify our holding any of those propositions. Short of our evolving sonar abilities of our own, we are cognitively closed off from such facts. Yet, contrary to PT, such facts clearly could exist.

Secondly, even if we put such radical examples aside, there remains a problem for PT with propositions about the physical world that we can grasp. Consider such propositions as the following:

(a)   It rained on this spot 15,000 years ago to the day.

(b)   The number of stars in the universe at this moment is odd.

Neither of these propositions is beyond our "cognitive reach"; each makes sense to us. Further, each is a proposition for which we can imagine the general sort of evidence needed to confirm or deny them: both (a) and (b), after all, are formally the same as propositions that we do evaluate every day (e.g., "It rained here last week"). What *is* difficult to imagine is how *we* (or anyone like us) could ever come into possession of the relevant evidence for (a) and (b)—even at the ideal limit of inquiry.[5]

These examples illustrate one half of a basic dilemma for a theory like PT. The dilemma, in essence, hangs on two different interpretations of "ideal epistemic conditions." The first half of the dilemma is what we've just seen: if "ideal epistemic conditions" are understood (as we've been understanding them so far) as conditions under which a cognitive agent much like ourselves would have all the relevant evidence that agent could have for or against a given proposition, then there will be many propositions that will never be justified or unjustified even in such conditions. PT would therefore entail that these same propositions are neither true nor false. Yet this seems to be the wrong result for (a) and (b), in view of the obvious relation these propositions bear to propositions that we do think capable of truth or falsity. Why should (a), for instance, be any less true or false than the proposition that it rained on this spot *ten* years ago?[6]

On the other hand, we could always interpret "ideal epistemic circumstances" as meaning those conditions under which a superior being has all the evidence it could have for or against a proposition. That is, we could take it that ideal epistemic circumstances are those circumstances in which evidence for *every proposition or its negation* is available. This is the other half of the dilemma, for strengthening ideal conditions in this way has its own problems. First, it would make ideal epistemic conditions the same for each proposition, for to talk of such conditions is to talk of having all the evidence for or against every proposition. This means that the ideal epistemic conditions for the belief that there is a table in the room are the same as they would be for the belief that there is life on Mars. This is not only implausible; it is a view that Putnam explicitly rejects (1989, 115; 1990, viii). Second, it would surely make ideal epistemic justification beyond the cognitive reach of creatures like us, for how plausible is it that even when we are as epistemically well situated as humans could be, we will have knowledge of *every* event in the past? Finally, to take it that ideal epistemic conditions are those in which we have justification for every proposition or its negation threatens to make the epistemic account trivial. For it begins to sound as if one has just snuck truth back into the account by declaring that the ideal epistemic situation is one in which all facts (that is, all truths) are available.

To sum up, the advocate of PT can interpret "ideal epistemic circumstances" weakly or strongly. If she interprets them weakly, as being the ideal epistemic conditions for agents like us, then since neither (a) nor (b) would be justified or unjustified in such conditions, neither is true or false. On the other hand, she can interpret "ideal conditions" strongly, but that makes ideal epistemic conditions into a unique and alien circumstance and ends up sneaking truth back into the account. Either way, the result is that truth can't be ideal justification.

Although the above objections are sufficient all by themselves to destabilize PT, I think that a third problem bears mentioning, since it revolves around the issue of whether theories will *converge* to the truth under PT. On the surface, it would seem that they do. Indeed, Putnam (1981) notes that there are two "key ideas" to his theory of truth. The first is that truth is independent of present justification but not of all justification; the second is that truth is expected to be stable or "convergent"; if both a statement and its negation could be "justified," even if conditions were as ideal as one could hope to make them, there is no sense in thinking of the statement as *having* a truth-value. (1981, 56)

The requirement of convergence here seems quite plausible. Convergence is plausible because we naturally expect truth to obey the principle that no proposition can be both true and false. Given this intuition, it is natural to assume that if truth is idealized justification, then just as no proposition can be both true and false, so no proposition can be ideally justified and ideally unjustified. Furthermore, we expect a proposition to count as "justified" only if there is more evidence in its favor than in favor of its negation. So if one thinks that truth is ideal justifiability, then propositions and their negations that are "equally coherent at the ideal limit" could be neither true nor false, neither justified nor unjustified, since the evidence is in favor of neither one nor the other.

But is an advocate of PT allowed to embrace convergence? A number of considerations would indicate a negative answer. First off, as Alston (1996, 198) notes, what counts as evidence for a proposition is relative to background assumptions. Whether I accept your data often depends on whether I accept the theoretical assumptions your experiments were based on. What propositions are taken as given? Are the pronouncements of certain individuals or certain books never questioned? What makes some facts relevant to the process of assessing the epistemic status of a proposition, and what makes others irrelevant? Questions like these point to the differences that can arise between what Alston sometimes calls "doxastic practices,"—or the ways we have in forming our beliefs. But if questions of justification are relative in this way, how can we expect convergence under ideal epistemic conditions?

This last point indicates what some readers may have already noticed: Putnam's desire to make PT subject to convergence seems in conflict with PT's alleged compatibility with metaphysical pluralism. For the pluralist is committed to saying that there could be statements or propositions, such as "There are exactly seven objects in the bag" and "There are not exactly seven objects in the bag," that are *both true*. Now to say that claims are *true* on PT is to say that they are ideally justified. Yet here we have Putnam declaring that it is a "key idea" of PT that cases like the one involving our friends Smith and Johnson, where both claims would intuitively be justified at the ideal limit, are cases where *neither* claim could be true (or false)! To put the matter in terms of epistemic theory, the problem is that the principle underlying convergence (namely that no statement and its negation can both be ideally justified) is in direct conflict with the pluralist intuition that some inconsistent propositions can be ideally justified. So Putnam's views on truth would seem to be less compatible with pluralism than they might seem at first blush.

There are, of course, ways to reconcile the apparent contradiction in Putnam's view. One way would interpret Putnam as holding that the "key idea" behind PT is that only *within or internal to a scheme* can propositions not be both ideally justified and ideally unjustified. This aligns with many of Putnam's other remarks and allows for the possibility that *two* schemes (one of which includes p and the other $\sim p$) are equally ideally coherent. But it entails the undesirable conclusion that there are two sorts of justification/coherence for Putnam and, by implication, two sorts of truth. The first type works internally to a scheme and admits of convergence: as he says, no proposition and its negation can both be true, or ideally justified. The second type works externally to a scheme and defies convergence, and hence allows for a "certain pluralism" with regard to schemes. This resolves the contradiction, all right, but at a serious price, for it leaves Putnam with the difficult problem of saying what it is that both sorts of truth share in common that makes *each a kind of truth.*

Of course, a metaphysical pluralist who wished to still cling to a version of PT might simply abandon Putnam's convergence requirement. Such a view would still have to face the other objections we discussed, however. Far better, it seems, to look for another way of understanding the pluralist idea of incompatible truths and for another theory of truth that avoids the grave problems of PT.

5.3 Antirealism about Truth: Deflationary Theories

As the name indicates, "deflationary" views of truth deflate the lofty pretensions of more "robust" theories of truth, such as the correspondence and epistemic theories. These latter types of theories purport to tell us the "essential nature" of truth—what truth really is. In contrast, deflationary theories dismiss the problem of the inner nature of truth as a pseudoproblem. There is no "problem of the nature of truth" because there is nothing picked out by the words "true" or "truth" that could have a nature.

In fact, the term "deflationism" actually marks out a whole family of views, linked by the metaphysical thesis that truth is not a property and differentiated by semantic views about the "real" meaning or function (in the deflationist's mind) of the concept of truth. Regardless of the details, all deflationist views have two basic aspects: their *ontological aspect* (truth is not a property) and their *semantic aspect* (what is said about the meaning or linguistic function of the word "true"). In other words, deflationists acknowledge that while the predicate "true" may have some function or other, it does not pick out a real feature of our beliefs, propositions, or sentences.

Even the deflationist admits that at first glance it looks *as if* truth is a property, whether it be of beliefs or sentences or propositions. For we often claim that this or that belief, this or that proposition, is true. And when we claim that something is *F*, we usually take this to mean that the something in question has a certain property, "*F*". But, of course, appearances can be misleading, as in the case of "exist," which also looks as if it might express a property, until we realize that it cannot, since existence is a necessary presupposition of having a property. The deflationist claims that the "surface grammar" of "true" is similarly misleading: it makes us think that there is a property of truth when there isn't. But how do we know that truth isn't a property? In this respect, the chief deflationist insight, which is variously accredited to Ramsey (1927), Frege (1892), or even Tarski (1944), is that the following sort of schemata strongly suggest deflationism:

T-SCHEMA   *The proposition that p is true if, and only if, p.*

DS   *"S" is true if, and only if, S.*

The first, our old friend the T-schema, is concerned with propositions. As I've remarked before (section 1.5), it should be taken as a necessary truth. But it is the second schema, which deals with sentences and is often called the "disquotational schema," that is most often associated with deflationism. The rough idea in either case is that a sentence or proposition, such as "Snow is white" (to again use that most overused example in all of philosophy), already contains the necessary and sufficient conditions for its truth. "Snow is white" is true just when snow is white. There isn't anything more that we need to say. And this, according to the deflationist, shows us that there really isn't a property of truth.

Exactly *why* it shows this varies from theorist to theorist, however. Sometimes it is said that DS illustrates that to assert that a statement is true is *semantically equivalent* to simply asserting the statement. According to F. P. Ramsey (1927, 36), the sentence "It is true that Caesar was murdered" means nothing more than the sentence "Caesar was murdered." To Ramsey, "is true" is "an obviously superfluous addition" to the original assertion (1927, 37). Therefore, we only *appear* to ascribe a property to a sentence or proposition when we say that it is true; in reality, we are ascribing nothing and are saying nothing more than if we had simply stated the proposition itself. Ascriptions of truth to statements, sentences, or propositions—as far as meaning or content are concerned—are "redundant." Other writers place less stress on Ramsey's thesis of "semantic equivalence" and stick to emphasizing what is sometimes called the "disquotational" aspect of DS, namely that the predicate "true," at least in many cases, can be taken as "removing" the quotation marks around a given sentence. This needn't be taken as showing that the two halves of an instance of DS are semantically equivalent or synonymous, as Ramsey believed. Rather, the point we are supposed to understand is simply that whatever can be said *with* the predicate can always be said *without* it. And this too is meant to underwrite the claim that when we assert that some statement is true, we are not ascribing a property, "truth," to the statement.

If the word "true" does not pick out a property of statements, propositions, or the like, then what function does it serve? This is the semantic aspect of deflationism, and we find a variety of answers. According to P. F. Strawson's *performative* theory (1950), for instance, apparent ascriptions of truth to statements or propositions are actually nonassertoric performative utterances. When I say "I promise to . . . ," for example, I am not describing anything, but rather I am performing a certain act. In the same way, the performative view holds, when I say, "It is true that the door is open," I am not describing but performing an act. Specifically, I am endorsing or agreeing to the claim that the door is open. The truth predicate acts as a device for the endorsement of statements or propositions. A second theory, deriving perhaps from Quine (1970, 11–12) is that the point of the truth predicate is purely formal, in this sense: it allows us to generalize over sentences or statements via "semantic ascent." By using the predicate "true," we can say simply that every statement of the form "*p* or not *p*" *is true*, without having to separately assert every statement of that form. Further still, the predicate allows us to generalize over propositions without knowing for sure which propositions we are generalizing over, as when we say, "Everything Socrates said was true." As it is sometimes put, the point of the predicate on this view is to allow us to make "blind ascriptions" of truth (Williams 1976, Horwich 1990). Without a predicate like "true," we would have to employ clumsy logical machinery like substitutional quantification to accomplish these tasks.

Michael Williams sums up the deflationist attitude this way:

> When we have pointed to certain formal features of the truth-predicate (notably its "disquotational" feature) and explained why it is useful to have a predicate like this (e.g., as a device for asserting infinite conjunctions), we have said just about everything there is to be said about truth." (1988, 424)

Deflationism, of whatever form, amounts to saying (as Ramsey so bluntly put it), "There is no separate problem of truth but merely a linguistic muddle" (1927, 142).

Expert readers will doubtless (and correctly) notice that my exposition has been quite brisk concerning the details of the various deflationary views, and I have not even mentioned some of the more technical variants.[7] My reason for this is that while a discussion of the pros and cons of the numerous types of deflationism is important, it is not necessary in the context of the present essay.[8] What concerns us primarily is whether any form of deflationism would make a good partner for metaphysical pluralism.

It is more difficult than one might suspect to find an advocate of *both* metaphysical pluralism and the deflationary view of truth.[9] A natural candidate for such a position would seem to be W. V. Quine, who often appears to push views akin to both "deflationism" and "metaphysical pluralism." According to Quine, *ontology is relative* in that "it makes no sense to say what the objects of a theory are, beyond saying how to interpret or reinterpret that theory into another" (1969, 50). There is no way to say what objects exist (according to a theory) without relying further on a "background theory" (Quine 1969, 52). This sounds very much like metaphysical pluralism. Furthermore, Quine would seem to advocate (and many writers interpret him as advocating) deflationism. For instance, he says, "To say that the statement 'Brutus killed Caesar' is true . . . is in effect simply to say that Brutus killed Caesar" (1960, 24). This certainly smacks of deflationism. On the surface, then, it would appear that Quine represents the sort of view we are looking for.

But the matter is complicated (as it always is when one is interpreting Quine). First off, despite his stance on ontological relativity, Quine is also one of contemporary philosophy's most steadfast advocates of global materialism. This is what leads Putnam, the archpluralist, to assert that Quine has rejected pluralism in the latter half of his career:

In [Quine's] early lecture "On What There Is," material objects were described as "posits" and even as "myths." . . . But from the "The Scope and Language of Science" and "Epistemology Naturalized" onward, Quine's claim has been that physics and physics alone gets to . . . "the true and ultimate nature of reality." (1994a, 482–483)

Furthermore, the many writers who ascribe deflationism to Quine do so on the basis of not only his Ramsey-like remarks such as the one I quoted above but also his clear advocacy of Tarski's "semantic theory" of truth. Yet not everyone agrees, to say the least, that Tarski's theory should be understood as a form of deflationism, and hence not everyone may agree that Quine is a deflationist either.[10] So just what Quine's views *are* with regard to truth and metaphysical pluralism would seem to be a matter for dispute.

Luckily, I think we can bypass the entire issue of who does or does not advocate both pluralism and deflationism. For, I think, there is an excellent case to be made that once one has adopted metaphysical pluralism, a deflationary view about truth is unmotivated. A pluralist might still adopt deflationism, but if I am right, there will be little reason for doing so.

To see this, let us return for a moment to the reason deflationists give for thinking that truth is not a property in the first place. As I understand the matter, deflationists hold that truth is not a property, because either (as DS supposedly shows) to assert that a statement is true is semantically equivalent to asserting the statement or, more cautiously (and again as DS "shows"), whatever can be said with the predicate "true" can be said without it. Now, someone unfamiliar with the drift of analytic philosophy in the last fifty years might be puzzled by this "argument" for deflationism. Why, they might wonder, does the fact (if it is a fact) that everything one says with the predicate "true" one can say without that same predicate provide any evidence whatsoever for thinking that the predicate fails to pick out a genuine property? Why should we think that the concept of truth is gratuitous simply because we can dispense with the *word* "true"?

As Kirkham has noted (1992, 330), this question reveals that the argument for deflationism has a hidden premise. The deflationist must be assuming that we should count a predicate as "genuine" only if we cannot eliminate it from our discourse without severely impairing our ability to express what we wish or need to say. Conversely, if we can eliminate the truth predicate and still say whatever we wish (even in the most hypothetical sense of "can"), then there is no need to think that it expresses a property, as opposed to merely acting as a device for endorsement or generalization. It is worth noting that the root idea here is the same whether one is examining nouns or predicates. Consider a statement like "I did it for John's sake," and suppose that I am worried about having to admit "sakes" into my ontology. According to philosophical orthodoxy, I can avoid the troublesome ontological commitment simply by paraphrasing the first statement into an equivalent statement that does not mention "sakes"—such as "I did it for John." In the same fashion, the deflationist claims that I need not worry about a property being expressed by "true" if I can paraphrase statements containing "true" into statements that do not contain "true." In both cases I am relieved of a bothersome ontological commitment by appealing to the expressive resources of my language.

I do not think that we should be convinced by this "paraphrase argument" on the part of the deflationist. First, as I pointed out in the last chapter, there is an obvious problem with taking paraphrase as a device for relieving us of ontological commitments. The problem is that the simple fact that I can paraphrase statements that appear to refer to *F*s into statements that do not appear to refer to *F*s doesn't by itself tell me *which* of these appearances I should take seriously. As Alston has pointed out, to give a paraphrase of p by citing q amounts to claiming that p and q have the same content, and having the same content is a symmetrical relation. As he adds, "Why shouldn't we say that the equivalence shows that when we assert [an instance of the T-schema] we are really, contrary to surface appearances, attributing the property of truth to a proposition?" (1996, 49). Why not, indeed.

In thinking about this question, it may help to briefly consider the reasons one might have for taking an "eliminativist" stand toward any sort of property as the deflationist does toward truth. Consider again the property of being a sake or sakehood. A deflationist might point out (in response to the point just above) that no one complains about paraphrasing *that* property away. "If you are right," our deflationist might add, "a defender of sakehood could reply to our paraphrase by simply saying that, e.g., 'I did it for John' only *appears not* to be about sakes! But this is absurd, because there are no sakes!" Quite right, there are no sakes. But the reason that we don't think that there are any sakes, and thus the reason we think that we can "paraphrase" them away, is quite different from the reasons the deflationist has for trying the same move with truth. The difference is that a lack of belief in sakes or sakehood is not a matter of theory, while a lack of belief in the property of truth is. Think of it in this way: If you ask a person on the street whether there are sakes (and hence whether there is the property of being a sake), they are apt to look at you strangely, for to talk of John's sake is, at the level of ordinary language, a *façon de parler*. But the reverse is the case with regard to truth (and falsity). Ask a person on the street if there are true beliefs and false beliefs, and they are apt to look at you strangely all right, but only because you seem to be doubting the obvious. If we are in a "linguistic muddle" about truth, as Ramsey believed, our reasons for thinking so can't be simple intuition. We must already have some antecedent reason for believing that a property like truth is ontologically suspect. The moral of the story isn't that paraphrase itself is useless, but that it can only be used to confirm what we believe we already know by other means.

So what are the other means by which one "knows" that truth is not a property? One reason that might be (and often is) cited by deflationists is that all other theories of truth are false, incoherent, or just plain no good. Maybe, but to push this reason to believe in deflationism is to beg the question at this point in the dialectic, for we are precisely on the search for positive reasons for thinking that truth is not a property. And believing that all the other theories are bad is not such a positive reason.

The only remaining alternative would seem to be one implicit in most theories of deflationism. Truth simply doesn't seem to be a respectable property from the perspective of a global naturalism or materialism. This was certainly the motivation for such views in Ramsey's and Tarski's day, when the logical positivists waged war on concepts that could not be reduced or defined in acceptably physicalist or scientific terms. And if the more radical methods of the positivists have been widely abandoned, certainly their unfailing loyalty to materialism and some form of empiricism has not. Thus we often find truth disparaged as a "nonnatural" or "metaphysical" notion by the contemporary deflationist. For consider: If the one true story of the world refers only to physical objects and their properties and a "reduction" of truth to these low-level properties is untenable, then there must be no property of truth. Similarly, if, broadly speaking, the "scientific method" is the one and only right way to gain knowledge about the world and scientific research can tell us nothing about the nature of truth and skepticism is untenable, then it would seem that there cannot be a property of truth. The point is this: deflationism, as a view about the nature of truth, makes good sense from the standpoint of an absolutist interpretation of the twin views of empiricism in epistemology and materialism in metaphysics. But, of course, from the standpoint of metaphysical pluralism, global materialism is simply one metaphysic of "ultimate reality" among many possible metaphysics. Once absolutism is given up, there is no longer any reason to think that the world *must* be described only in physical terms, and thus there is no longer any reason to think that science is the only true way to acquire knowledge.

So the chief motivation for taking the deflationist project seriously is simply not going to be compelling to a metaphysical pluralist. Of course, nothing I've said would prevent a metaphysical pluralist from adopting the deflationary metaphysic about truth—pluralists are entitled to their own opinions on metaphysical issues, just like everyone else. But there is nothing about *pluralism* that would force or even motivate such a view.

5.4   The Correspondence Theory and Pluralism

Like the other theories we've looked at, correspondence accounts of truth come in different shapes and sizes. But the core of any correspondence theory is the following idea:

CT   *The proposition that p is true if, and only if, the proposition that p corresponds to reality.*

According to CT, there are three metaphysical aspects to any true proposition: the proposition itself (the truth bearer), its correspondence (the truth relation), and the reality to which it corresponds (the truth maker). Roughly speaking, a proposition is made true, according to CT, by its relation to an actual, obtaining reality. So if we continue to assume that propositions are the bearers of truth, there are two remaining issues that need to be understood if we are to understand CT. The first is the nature of the truth relation; the second is the nature of the truthmaker.

Various suggestions have been made for the latter role, but the most dominant, and certainly the most intuitive from the standpoint of ordinary language, is the notion of a fact. Typically, we take it that a proposition is true because of its relation to facts. It is facts that make thoughts true. If so, then we might take it that adopting CT amounts to endorsing instances of the following schema:

CT*   *The proposition that p is true if, and only if, the proposition that p corresponds to some fact.*[11]

In other words, propositions are true when they correspond to the facts. Of course, one might wonder in turn what a "fact" is. One initially attractive response to such a demand would be to *identify* facts with true propositions. To do so would be to embrace what could be called the "identity theory" of truth:

IT   *The proposition that p is true if, and only if, it is identical to some fact.*[12]

In other words, the proposition that *p* is true when it is the fact that *p*. This is the sort of view that John McDowell would seem to endorse when he says,

There is no ontological gap between the sort of thing one can mean, or generally the sort of thing one can think, and the sort of thing that can be the case. When one thinks truly, what one thinks *is* what is the case. (1994, 27)

Is IT a realist view of truth? At first glance, it may seem that the answer to this question depends on how we interpret IT itself. When a philosopher or scientist makes an identity claim, for example, "Water is H_2O," it is usually thought that one of the terms in the claim is meant to be more explanatory of the phenomenon in question than the other. In other words, in the present example, "H_2O" is more revealing of the nature of that stuff that fills our lakes than "water"; hence "H_2O" has *explanatory priority*. Whether IT is taken as a realist view of truth seems to depend on which term, "proposition" or "fact," has the explanatory priority. If it is "proposition" and propositions are taken to be mental entities (such as "thoughts"), then to say that facts are true propositions smacks of idealism. This in turn might seem to tell against interpreting IT as a realist view of truth in my sense. In truth, however, it does not. For suppose that we take propositions, and thus facts, as mental entities. That means that the existence of propositions (and hence facts) will depend on minds. But it doesn't imply that a proposition's *being a fact* depends on our minds, and it is the latter that IT takes to be the essence of truth. On the other hand, if it is "facts" that have the upper hand from an explanatory view and facts are entities of the external world, then IT does not stand as a barrier to one's being a realist in any sense. Thus, one could still be a realist about truth (in my two-pronged sense) and hold IT. But it would not be accurate to call IT a correspondence theory of truth, since according to CT, correspondence is a two-place relation, while identity is a one-place relation. Simply put, according to IT, there are not two things that "correspond" with one another but only one thing, which we can call either a "true proposition" or a "fact."

Of course, there are reasons against identifying facts with true propositions that the traditional correspondence theorist could marshal in her favor. For example, the fact that the butler's prints are on the murder weapon can certainly cause one to suspect him of the crime, but no proposition (true or false) can cause anything. Second, many facts presumably exist independently of human beings, but it is arguable, at least, that propositions do not. In any event, in chapter 1, I suggested that as far as this book went, I was not going to be offering an ontological "theory" of facts, other than simply assuming them to be equivalent to obtaining states of affairs. Thus I take it that to talk of the fact that there is a tree outside my window is to speak of the *obtaining state of affairs* that there is a tree outside my window. And the obtaining of *that* state of affairs is what makes my thought that there is a tree outside my window true. Once we look at facts in this manner, we can elaborate a bit on schema CT* as follows:

CT**   *The proposition that p is true if, and only if, the proposition that p corresponds to the state of affairs that p and p obtains.*

Of course, a correspondence theorist who feels the need to have a more robust theory of facts need not collapse facts and states of affairs together (although if she doesn't, she needs to explain why we should separate them). In any event, in what follows I shall take CT to involve a commitment to facts.

Let us turn to the question of the correspondence relation itself. George Pitcher, writing in the 1960s, distinguished two sorts of views on the correspondence relation: *correspondence as correlation* and *correspondence as congruence* (1964, 9–11). The latter sort of theory is perhaps the most well known, having been advocated by Russell (1912) and the early Wittgenstein (1922). On this theory, a relation of "structural isomorphism" obtains between facts and propositions. Pitcher (1964, 10) compared this type of correspondence to that which obtains between two halves of a torn piece of paper: the two halves are structured so that they exactly fit one another. Thus, on this view, a true proposition is one that "pictures" or "fits" an actual fact, while a false proposition fits no fact at all. The other sort of correspondence, "correlation," is the sort of theory found in Austin 1950. According to this line, every proposition is related to some fact or state of affairs; if that fact is actual (if the state of affairs obtains), the proposition in question is true; if not, the proposition is false. The relation here, however, is not structural: facts and propositions don't "fit" one another the way a hand fits a glove; rather, they correspond in the same way that the first name in the Chicago phone book may "correspond" to the first name in the Memphis phone book, simply in virtue of the fact that they are both the "first name in the phone book." Specifically, facts, on the correlation view, don't make their corresponding propositions true in virtue of a one-to-one match between the fact's component parts and the proposition's component parts, and between those parts' structural relations to each other. Rather, facts and propositions relate as whole units.

These were pretty much the only two alternatives for correspondence theorists for most of this century. These days, however, the correspondence theory of truth has taken on a different look altogether. This is the theory of *correspondence as causal relation*. The view has two aspects. First, following Davidson (1967) and Field (1972), these theorists maintained that the concept of truth for natural languages can be understood by a Tarskian recursive definition. Roughly speaking, sentences of the form "*a* is *F*" are true in virtue of the fact that there exists an object that "*a*" designates and that is among the objects "*F*" applies to. In other words, the truth of a sentence consists in the *reference* of its parts to an objective reality. The second aspect of the theory takes the reference relation itself to be a physical or causal relation between words and the world. In short, a statement or sentence token (a particular use of a sentence) is true, on this theory, if its component parts bear an appropriate causal relation to certain objects in the world.

As one would suspect, each of these views on correspondence have their advantages and disadvantages (see Kirkham 1992, 119–130; Pitcher, 1964; Devitt 1984, 26–28). But for our purposes, the relative merits of each view are irrelevant, since each view is demonstrably consistent with metaphysical pluralism. Once we've understood the nature of pluralism and the correspondence theory of truth, the argument for this claim is quite brief.

The central doctrines of metaphysical pluralism, as I've understood that view here, are what I called fact and content relativity. That is, facts and propositions are both relative to conceptual schemes. CT is clearly consistent with these doctrines: if either sense of correspondence described above makes sense, then *relative* facts and *relative* propositions can correspond to one another in either way. Thus a pluralist could adopt a "correspondence as congruence" theory, as follows:

CP   *The proposition that p-relative-to-C is true if, and only if, the proposition that p-relative-to-C is structurally isomorphic with the fact that p-relative-to-C.*

Similarly for a "correspondence as correlation" theory. Even the "correspondence as causal relation" theory is consistent with metaphysical pluralism. Advocates of that view tend to take sentences, and particularly sentence tokens, as the primary bearers of truth. Nonetheless, most causal theorists would accept CT's reliance on propositional truth if glossed in the right way. For instance, we might identify propositions with classes of interpreted sentences. Thus, the proposition that grass is green could be identified with the class of sentences that can be used to assert that grass is green. Similarly CT's talk of "facts" can be understood by the causal theorist as a clumsy way of talking about objects having certain properties. Propositional truth can then be understood as derived from sentential truth, and CT can be glossed as follows:

CT*** *"S", under interpretation I, is true if, and only if, "S" (under that interpretation) corresponds to some fact.*

Here "S" corresponds to some fact just when its component parts bear appropriate reference relations to certain objects in the world. In the case of a sentence of the form "x is F," this will mean that what "x" denotes, under the interpretation in question, has the property that F designates, under the same interpretation.[13] And, of course, reference, denotation, and designation are all to be understood as causal relations between words, objects, and properties. The metaphysical pluralist can still accept CT***, for fact and content relativity can be stated without talking about "facts" or "content" (propositions). Under the present line of thought, fact relativism amounts to saying that objects have the properties they do only relative to a conceptual scheme. Similarly, content relativism is the view that sentential interpretations are relative to conceptual schemes, which is to say that interpretations are indeterminate unless they are relative to a conceptual scheme. The world does not interpret sentences for us; for the pluralist, independent of conceptual schemes there is literally no fact of the matter about the reference of our terms. Now suppose that we understand the sentence token "Grass is green" under an interpretation that takes it to express that grass is green. The pluralist will hold this interpretation to be relative to a particular conceptual scheme. If so, then the pluralist is still free to believe that the sentence "Grass is green" (under the C-relative interpretation) is true in virtue of the fact that "grass" is causally related to grass in C, and "green" is causally related to greenness in C, and grass actually is green in C. In other words, pluralism is consistent with the view that internal to a conceptual scheme, words are causally related to the objects they refer to and it is in virtue of this fact that sentences are true or false.

In sum, there is no logical incoherence in supposing that facts and propositions are relative to conceptual schemes and that truth is the correspondence of (relative) propositions with (relative) facts.

Of course, if *this* were all there was to say about the relation between realism about truth and metaphysical pluralism, the reader would be right to feel cheated. Logical compatibility, while significant, is a far cry from pragmatic or *real* compatibility. As Linda Alcoff writes,

> One could still conceptualize true statements as those that correspond to the facts, where facts are understood as partly determined by conceptual schemes. This is certainly possible, but a correspondence theory of truth is drained of its metaphysical content by such an approach. Given the historical associations of correspondence with classical realism . . . , such a move would also be misleading. (1996, 175)

By saying that a correspondence theory of truth would be "drained of its metaphysical content" if combined with a view like metaphysical pluralism, Alcoff is indicating that the correspondence theory is typically associated with absolutism (in my preferred jargon). That is, the facts that the correspondence theorist matches with propositions are generally thought to be unique, absolute facts—facts that are not relative to conceptual schemes. There is a reason for this association of correspondence and absolutism. Even if, as I have argued, the correspondence theory of truth does not entail metaphysical absolutism (because it is consistent with pluralism), some fairly simple considerations seem likely to lead a metaphysical absolutist to adopt the correspondence theory of truth. For the absolutist, the totality of facts and propositions is unique and determinate. There is only one set of facts for our conceptual schemes and worldviews to represent. Hence, in view of the obvious plurality of conflicting worldviews, it would be bizarre to think that truth and fact were relative to our worldviews or the conceptual schemes they contain. On the basis of these considerations, it seems that the metaphysical absolutist, if she is to have any theory of truth at all, will be driven in the direction of the correspondence theory of truth—a theory that takes truth as a direct relation between fact and thought. Furthermore, the view of concepts that underlies absolutism implies that the correspondence in question is itself determinate. This sort of consideration is apparently what led Putnam recently to define "metaphysical realism" (the view he takes himself to be opposing) as "the view that truth involves a fixed correspondence (a correspondence relation which is one and the same no matter what sort of statement is under consideration) to a fixed set of 'objects' and 'properties' (1994a, v). Thus, because of the close and apparently natural association between the correspondence theory of truth and absolutism, it appears that Alcoff is right: it would be misleading to say that the pluralist can adopt a correspondence theory of truth *as that theory is traditionally conceived by its advocates*. Nonetheless, the logical compatibility of correspondence with pluralism remains significant, for it shows that there remains room for a theory of truth that is at once realist and amenable to pluralism. It suggests that a more pluralist-friendly realism about truth (a theory that is nonepistemic and nondeflationary) might still be constructed. But what sort of theory would this be?

For starters, a realist *cum* pluralist theory of truth cannot be pinned down to any particular metaphysical view, for metaphysical pluralism demands that there can be more than one true story of the "ultimate nature" of things—even of the ultimate nature of truth. Thus a pluralist view of truth must be metaphysically *thin* without being metaphysically *invisible*, like the deflationist theory. In other words, the conception in question must be at once both *fluid* and *stable*. Fluid because the nature of truth must be amenable to multiple explanations, yet stable because the pluralist must also retain a notion of truth that remains constant in some respects across conceptual schemes. Without such stability, she could not say that some propositions are true in more than one scheme and some are not. Finally, this theory must do all of the above without ending up rejecting realism about truth.

5.5   Minimal Realism about Truth

I began this chapter by noting that minimally speaking, a proposition is true in the realist sense when the world is as that proposition says it is. Call this *minimal realism* about truth. As Mark Johnston has noted,

The notion of truth is a Minimalist paradigm, at least in this sense: although in using the notion ordinary practitioners are thereby using an [objective, nonepistemic] notion, it is none the less a metaphysically austere notion. (1993a, 111)

A minimal realism of this sort has been discussed sympathetically by Johnston (1993a), Wright (1992), and Van Cleve (1996), but it is William

Alston (1996) who has developed the position in the greatest detail. According to Alston,

What it takes to make a statement true on the realist conception is the actual obtaining of what is claimed to obtain in making that statement. If what is stated is that grass is green then it is grass's *being* green that is both necessary and sufficient for the truth of the statement. Nothing else is relevant. (1996, 7)

In particular, it is not relevant that anyone believe, justifiably or not, that grass is green in order for that proposition to be true. For Alston, the T-schema itself can be taken as illuminating, if not defining, minimal realism about truth: "If we understand that any T-statement [any instance of the T-schema] is conceptually, analytically true, true by virtue of the meanings of the terms involved, in particular the term 'true,' then we thereby understand what it is for a proposition to be true" (1996, 27). Indeed, if we combine the T-schema with the intuitive principle that things are as the proposition that p says they are if, and only if, p, we get MR (minimal realism):

MR   *The proposition that p is true if, and only if, things are as the proposition that p says they are.*

But even without accepting the additional premise, Alston is surely right that one can plausibly read the T-schema itself as suggestive of MR, or the view that truth is a nonepistemic property of propositions. And what else does a realist theory of truth really need?

To take instances of the T-schema and MR as conceptual truths is not to embrace the "redundancy theory." That is, it does not entail that truth is not a property or that "p" and "the proposition that p is true" are synonymous. The minimal realist can hold that instances of the T-schema are *weak conceptual truths*. On this view, the two halves of a T-proposition are not identical in content, but they are necessarily equivalent (true in all the same worlds) in virtue of the concepts involved. Like Putnam, the Alstonian minimal realist forgoes trying to formally define truth; instead, the proposal is meant to be an informal elucidation of the concept of truth—one that relates the concept to other concepts and provides "particularly illuminating necessary and sufficient conditions for the application of a term without thereby providing a synonym for such an application" (Alston 1996, 35).

To return to the central point, if we grant that MR is qualified to be a realist theory (if not a traditional theory of that type), what makes it "minimal"? The answer is that MR lacks the specific metaphysical implications of its more robust cousin, the correspondence theory. As we've just seen above, correspondence theories typically involve certain assumptions about the nature of the correspondence relationship, propositions, and facts. In particular, the correspondence theory is usually taken as entailing an absolutely determinate structural relationship between propositions and scheme-independent facts. Minimal realism, on the other hand, remains neutral on the main metaphysical questions regarding truth. These same points makes MR particularly suitable for adoption by the metaphysical pluralist. In chapter 3, I discussed how the pluralist will understand the minimal use of our most (contextually) basic concepts to "float free" of competing metaphysical pictures. Indeed, I claimed that it is the minimalist character of these concepts that allows them to be shared across conceptual schemes that also employ more robust extensions of those same concepts. I shall argue that the pluralist can, and indeed should, treat truth the same way.

A minimalist concept of truth, in both Alston's sense and in the sense of "minimal" I was concerned with in chapter 3, is a metaphysically thin concept. In effect, this means that a minimalist concept of truth requires minimalist concepts of proposition and fact as well. If we take any instance of the T-schema as necessarily true (e.g., the proposition that the pool is open is true if, and only if, the pool is open), then there are propositions if there are any truths at all. But granting the existence of propositions doesn't force one to take a stand on their metaphysical nature. As in section 1.2, one can take "proposition" in the minimal sense as a functional concept; a proposition, in effect, is whatever stands to asserting and denying as numbers stand to adding and subtracting. Call this a *minimalist concept of propositions*. Propositions, in the minimal sense, are what occupy the role of the unquoted variable in the schema "s" says that p. Thus, the only constraint on propositions is formal: propositions are the objects of "that" clauses. Such a view is consistent with any metaphysical theory of propositions (including views that reduce propositions to classes of sentences) and with instrumentalist theories that claim that it is of value to talk *as if* there were separate entities over and above sentences uttered in specific contexts (Alston 1996, 19).[14]

The same story holds for facts. It would be difficult for the minimal realist to deny the F-schema:

F-SCHEMA   *It is a fact that p if, and only if, p.*

This, together with the T-schema, implies the following:

It is a fact that p if, and only if, it is true that p.

But again, the minimalist can remain neutral concerning the ontological status of facts. She can embrace a *minimalist view of facts*, according to which our concept of fact is nailed down by the F-schema: a fact is simply what is the case. The minimal realist can then accept that statements are made true by facts without that committing herself to a specific ontology of facts. For example, consider Berkeleyan idealism, according to which for *p* to be the case is for it to be an idea in some mind (perhaps the mind of God). Roughly speaking, all facts are mental facts. Idealism of this sort is completely compatible with minimal realism about truth, since the idealist's theory is not about truth but about reality, about the nature of facts. It is not any part of the minimal-realist position on the concept of truth to insist that facts must be ideas in the mind of God or external to all minds or reducible to ordered pairs of objects and properties or anything else. MR is committed to facts, but only minimal facts.

So MR, via minimalist concepts of proposition and fact, floats free of metaphysical debates over the nature of truth bearers and truth makers. But there is a third important metaphysical issue confronting any conception of truth: the nature of truth itself. In effect, this is the question of whether MR can remain neutral about the nature of the *property of truth*.[15]

One tactic to consider in this regard is Paul Horwich's idea that truth is a property but not a "substantive" property; that is, truth is not "an ordinary sort of property—a characteristic whose underlying nature will account for its relations to other ingredients of reality" (1990, 2). According to Horwich, "true" is unlike certain other predicates, such as "magnetic." Truth, unlike magnetism, has no deep underlying nature worth examining by science; it is not a *natural* property.

The problem with Horwich's position (at least as far as minimal realism is concerned) is that it is not actually neutral on the nature of the truth property. To imply that truth is not a natural property, unsuitable for empirical investigation, just *is* to take a metaphysical stand on the nature of truth. Furthermore, by refusing to allow that there is anything more to be said about the nature of truth, Horwich effectively embraces standard deflationism. Like standard deflationists, Horwich's underlying assumption is that the only properties worth discussing are natural properties capable of being investigated scientifically. Since truth is not such a property, he concludes that there is no "deep" theory of truth to be had. But as Alston (1996, 51) has pointed out, the minimal realist needn't accept this assumption. One can take a minimal stance toward the concept of truth without shutting the door on more substantive investigation of its nature.[16]

According to Alston, "deep theories" of the nature of truth are consistent with the minimalist conception because there is a sharp distinction between the property of truth and the concept of truth. The minimalist *concept* of truth is consistent with a substantive or nonsubstantive account of the *property*. Alston introduces the distinction by appealing to Putnam's and Kripke's view of natural kinds, which implies that kinds (or properties) may have certain features not reflected in the concept. Just as facts about gold or anger may outrun our ordinary concepts of gold or anger, so it may be with truth. Our concept of anger may be simple enough, but a physiological theory of the nature of anger may be a very complex matter indeed. In the same way, Alston argues, the property of truth may have aspects that our ordinary concept lacks.

At first glance, Alston's distinction between the concept and property of truth seems to be exactly the sort of distinction that the metaphysical pluralist requires if she is to adopt MR. The metaphysical pluralist, after all, must avoid saying that there is one true account of the nature of truth, and Alston's distinction would allow us to opt for a plurality of metaphysical accounts of the property even while maintaining one (metaphysically "thin") concept of truth. In short, it would seem to allow for *alethic* (truth) *pluralism*.

Crispin Wright is one of the few writers who has explicitly considered pluralism with regard to truth:

If the only essential properties of a truth predicate are *formal*—a matter of its use complying with certain very general axioms (platitudes)—then such predicates may or may not, in different areas of discourse, have a varying *substance*. (1992, 23)

Wright's own theory of truth bears some interesting similarities to MR. According to Wright, our concept of truth is minimally fixed by the T-schema (or its sentential cousin DS) and a series of "platitudes," such as that to assert is to present as true and that every proposition has a negation. Further, Wright argues that the T-schema itself entails that truth is a property and that it cannot be identified with simple justifiability—even justifiability in ideal conditions. But he is not quite as willing as Alston to concede that truth is never epistemic in any sense. Wright does want to allow that for some sorts of statements, truth might be understood as the epistemic property of "superassertibility"—durable justification that is never overridden. According to Wright, this means that the "truth predicate" can vary its substance from discourse to discourse, even while it abides by the T-schema and other minimal platitudes in every discourse.

Alethic pluralism along these lines is obviously attractive to the metaphysical pluralist.[17] Yet it is not entirely clear what Wright has in mind. His talk of "truth predicates" makes it sound as if he is saying that the words "truth" and "true" are ambiguous. But he sensibly rejects this interpretation elsewhere (Wright, 1995). So how *should* we understand alethic pluralism if it is not the view that "truth" is ambiguous?

This returns us (finally!) to the point: Armed with the distinction between concept and property, it would seem that we can make sense of alethic pluralism. Simply put, the minimal realist can hold that there is only one concept of truth but allow that there may be more than one property that fits the constraints marked out by the concept. In this way, the nature of truth can vary across conceptual schemes even as a single, univocal concept of truth is being shared in those same schemes. In short, it seems that if we combine Wright with Alston we get—voilà!—a realist pluralism about truth!

Unfortunately, the recipe won't quite work just as it is. Alston's distinction between the property and concept of truth is not as innocent as it may initially seem. Even if you think that there is a rough and ready distinction between concepts and properties in general, it doesn't follow that there must be a clear distinction *in this case*. The point is that the concept of truth is very different from the types of concepts that can be distinguished from the properties they represent. One can grasp the concept of gold without knowing much at all about the nature of gold; this is illustrated by the fact that an explanation of the concept of gold is quite a different thing from an explanation of its chemical nature. Similarly, in order to hang the minimalist hat on a distinction between the property and concept of truth, we should be able to distinguish, as we do in the case of gold, explanations of the concept and explanations of the property. The Alstonian minimalist owes us a story of how one might investigate the truth property independently of investigating the truth concept. But this story seems impossible to give. For consider: One might investigate the truth property, independently of investigating the truth concept, by a priori or a posteriori methods. To investigate something a priori is ultimately a matter of relying on one's fundamental intuitions. But how does one distinguish "intuitions" about the concept and intuitions about the property? Surely, there is no criterion that clearly separates the two. On the other hand, prospects seem dim for investigating the property of truth a posteriori. One tests for truth in the lab, but in doing so, it is not truth itself that is tested for but what one thinks is true. Truth itself is no more or less amenable to a posteriori investigation than logical necessity, identity, or existence. Therefore, even if there is some abstract or minimal distinction between the concept and property of truth, it appears unlikely to bear much theoretical weight.

Yet even if there isn't a clear distinction between the concept and property of truth as Alston believes, the suggestion implicit in his account is worth retaining: the property of truth may vary from context to context. We need only add that a single minimal concept of truth may vary as well, in the sense that it can be extended or enriched differently across contexts. In chapter 3, I discussed how some minimal concepts are also excellent examples of *fluid* concepts: they are subject to radically divergent extensions in use.[18] Two strikingly different and even incompatible "robust" concepts can both be enrichments of the same "thin" or minimal concept. That framework already provides a structure for understanding how our minimally realist account of truth could meet the demands spelled out at the end of section 5.4. There I claimed that for a realist view of truth to be truly compatible with metaphysical pluralism, it must be both fluid and stable. The minimally realist concept of truth meets the former demand, I shall argue, because it can be more or less enriched in distinct contexts. It meets the latter demand because even the most robust concepts of truth are extensions of the concept marked out by MR. Thus it might happen that in some contexts the appropriate concept of truth is only the minimally realist concept, while in other contexts, various robust enrichments of that concept could be in use. In these latter contexts, our theory of truth would be deeper and more substantive, as Wright suggests. And on this model, we can say this *without* relying on a sharp distinction between the concept and property of truth, for the subject of the more substantive theories would still be an enrichment of our minimally realist concept of truth. Further, since even robust concepts of truth have the minimalist concept as a necessary element, realist truth will be "preserved" across contexts. Logical inference is a function of our minimal concept of truth (as we would expect from the ubiquity of our basic logical concepts).

Our minimal concept of truth picks out those propositions that represent the world as it is. Representing the world accurately is just what true propositions do—it is their minimal function, in other words. But like any function, how that function is realized in some contexts may be different from how it is realized in others. Differences among contexts come in two relevant types: differences *between* conceptual schemes and differences *internal* to a single worldview or conceptual scheme.

In the recent literature, alethic pluralism is usually presented as a view according to which our concept of truth can vary across types of *discourse,* where a discourse is a particular region of our language distinguished by its content. Thus one finds philosophers distinguishing between "moral" and "physical object" discourse, and even between "comic" and "aesthetic" discourse. To my way of thinking, this should be understood as an alethic pluralism internal to a conceptual scheme. This is because one's conceptual scheme, in my preferred sense of that term, is the structured network comprised of *all* of one's concepts at a particular time. In turn, one's scheme is part of a worldview: the totality of one's attitudes, beliefs, cognitive capacities, implicit practices, and concepts. There are not separate moral, epistemological, and aesthetic conceptual schemes, but there are separate moral, epistemological, and aesthetic *concepts*. These different types of concepts give rise to different kinds of propositions—propositions that may be true in very different ways.

The suggestion is that MR is compatible with truth having a more than minimal nature in different parts of a conceptual framework. This is reminiscent of Wright's position mentioned above, but it is also related to a similar view developed by Terence Horgan in a series of papers on truth and semantics (1986, 1991, 1996).[19] According to Horgan, truth in any discourse has a certain minimal nature, what he calls "correct assertibility." To say that p is correctly assertible is *not* to say that it is justifiable in any sense. In Horgan's jargon, semantic norms are not reducible to epistemic norms. Nonetheless, "the contextually operative semantic norms governing correct assertibility (i.e., truth) can vary from one discourse to another in ways that bear on the discourse's proper ontological treatment" (1996, 992). On this picture, a statement will be correctly assertible on a robustly realist interpretation just when the norms in question are both *tight* (they "conspire with the world" to make the statements in question have determinate truth values) and *referentially strict* (the statements have direct language-to-world connections). Statements about our immediate perceptual environment, for example, would be robustly true by requiring a causal correspondence with the world. On the other hand, discourses are less robust to the extent to which their norms are less strict and less tight. Talk about theoretical entities such as corporations or concertos can be true without there being any direct causal relationship between our claims and certain abstract objects. Consider, for instance, the statement "Microsoft is a powerful corporation." Uttered in the appropriate context, this statement certainly has a truth value. Yet what Horgan calls the "referential norms" for this claim may be somewhat loose in our scheme. The world's contribution to the truth of the claim may be rather *indirect* in that there may be no direct causal contact between an object and our talk about it but only a more complicated relationship with certain legal and economic practices. If Horgan's suggestion is right, our propositions about corporations may still correspond to the world, but not in any direct causal sense.

Minimal realism about truth is also consistent with an even more antirealist interpretation of certain types of discourse. For another example, consider an aesthetic proposition, such as the following: "One of the more important themes in Shakespeare's *King Lear* is the ironic nature of human suffering."[20] Let us assume that we wish to take this statement as true. If we interpret "true" here as MR urges us to, then, independently of whether I or anyone agrees, it is the case (it is a fact, in other words) that the nature of suffering is an important theme of *King Lear*. Although this is clearly a matter of great dispute, it is tempting to take propositions of this sort to have *some* objective content. Certainly, the statement above is more plausible than one that claims that *Lear* is really about basket-weaving techniques in tenth-century China. But it also seems that the sense in which it is a fact (if it is) that *King Lear* is concerned with human suffering is a different sense in which it is a fact that AIDS is a life-threatening disease or that Microsoft is a powerful corporation. There is a softness in the former fact that seems absent in the latter two facts. One way to account for this intuition would be to adopt what Crispin Wright has called an "evidential constraint" in the aesthetic context:

EVIDENTIAL CONSTRAINT   *It is a fact that p only if it is justifiable that p.*

When we are concerned with aesthetic facts, and maybe even moral facts, it seems plausible to take them to be epistemically constrained. For if no one could ever defend or justify attributing a theme of suffering to *Lear*, it would be empty to assert that suffering is a theme of the play. (Similarly, one might hold that there could be no morally wrong acts that we could not *know* are morally wrong.) Of course, because of the conceptual connection between truth and fact, this evidential constraint ensures that in the aesthetic context all truths are justifiable. But it doesn't entail that the truth of propositions within that context *consists in* their being justifiable. The truth of the proposition about *Lear* can continue to consist, as MR would have it, in the ironic nature of human suffering being an important theme in Shakespeare's play. MR is consistent with an epistemic constraint on certain types of facts, and as a result, our realist concept of truth can be used in discourses that are epistemically constrained.

I have been discussing how one's concept of truth might be flexible *internal* to one's conceptual framework. The position allows for alethic pluralism *across* schemes as well. Just as with the concepts of mind or object, we can imagine the minimal concept of truth being extended differently in different schemes of concepts. For example, a globally materialist conceptual scheme would naturally employ the robustly realist concept of truth marked out by CT***. On the other hand, a classical or "absolute" idealist metaphysic could adopt a version of the identity theory of truth, according to which a thought is true just when it is identical to a thought of God's. And as with the concepts of mind and object, debates over the nature of truth are therefore substantive or not depending on whether we interpret them to be over the shared minimal concept of truth or judge them to be employing radically different extensions of that concept. In sum, truth can be doubly plural in context: within and across conceptual schemes.

I'll conclude this section by adding a brief remark on vagueness and the T-schema. The fluid picture of concepts that underlies pluralism implies that many concepts are vague. The use of such concepts can therefore lead to vague assertions. But one might wonder if the T-schema, or the obviously related principle MR, can handle such propositions. After all, if the proposition that p is indeterminate (neither true nor false), then what are we to make of the claim that it is true that p if, and only if, p? It is sometimes said that where "p" is indeterminate, "it is true that p" must be false, which therefore makes the T-proposition in question false as well. But this is counterintuitive. If it is indeterminate whether p, then it is surely not false that it is true that p, but *indeterminate*. If it is indeterminate whether my brother is bald, then it indeterminate whether it is true that my brother is bald. But this fact does not damage our acceptance of the T-schema or MR, since the component propositions of any of their instances will always receive the same truth value, whether that value be true, false, or indeterminate.[21]

No doubt, the above reasoning implies that there are not only vague and indeterminate propositions but also vague and indeterminate states of affairs. For according to MR, a proposition is true when what it says to be the case is the case, and in certain situations, what it says is going to be vague. While this may be a problem for the absolutist who thinks that states of affairs determinately obtain or don't obtain independently of any conceptualization, the possibility of vague states of affairs is no problem for the metaphysical pluralist. Relative to some conceptual scheme, whether x is a game may be an indeterminate state of affairs. If so, then whether x is a game will also be an indeterminate proposition relative to that scheme. But this will not surprise the pluralist, whose very position is predicated on a deep interconnection between concepts and the world.[22]

5.6 Relative Truth

There remains one last objection to my claim that pluralism is compatible with realism about truth. Namely, it seems as if pluralism implies that truth itself is relative. And relativism about truth itself is not only a problematic philosophical position, it is clearly at odds with minimal realism. According to MR, all that is required for a proposition to be true is for the world to be as that proposition says that it is. Nothing is mentioned about truth being relative.

The objection sounds plausible. After all, if one is a relativist about fact and content, how could one avoid relativism about truth? As Chris Swoyer has noted, the argument seems straightforward:

[For the pluralist] truth cannot reside in a correspondence with a neutral world of facts, for no such world exists. Truth does indeed involve the way the world is, but since this is relative to a framework, truth too is relative. (1982, 103)

Now the validity of this argument clearly depends on what is meant by saying that "truth is relative." On one interpretation, "truth is relative" means that our *concept of truth is a relative concept*. A relative concept of truth is one according to which true is analyzed as meaning *true-for*, a two-place relation with propositions as one relatum and persons, communities, cultures, or conceptual schemes as the other. This sort of view has two radical consequences. As the value of "x" changes, the meaning of "true-for-x" will shift, and hence the meaning of "true" itself will also change. Second, if we understand truth as truth-for-a-scheme, then the truth value of one and the same proposition can vary from scheme to scheme. Let us call any view that takes truth to be truth-for-a-scheme, *truth relativism*.

There are at least two reasons for the pluralist to avoid truth relativism. First, I've argued that the pluralist must retain a notion of truth that is *stable* across conceptual schemes if she is going to allow for cross-scheme evaluation. But a relative concept of truth is by definition unstable across schemes. Under a relative concept of truth, I can't literally say that minimally speaking, some proposition is true on both of our schemes. I might be able to say that the proposition that AIDS is a life-threatening disease is true-in-C and true-in-D and true-in-E, etc. But to do so would be to assert that the proposition that AIDS is a life-threatening disease has a (perhaps infinite) conjunctive property. Yet for it to have such a conjunctive property is surely different from it being *true*.

Second, what does "true-for-C" mean anyway? This clearly complex predicate contains as a component part the predicate "true." Therefore, to say that "true" means "true-for-C" is unhelpful unless we are told first what "true" means. But if we have a definition of "true" *already*, then it can't be right to say that "true" means "true-for-C," since in order to know what "true-for-C" means, we would need to know what "true" means. We would be arguing in a circle, and a small one at that.

So things don't look good if pluralism entails that truth is relative in the sense above. Fortunately, pluralism does not entail truth relativism. The only sense in which it does imply that truth is relative is trivial and has no bearing on realism. Recall that the argument is the following:

- Truth concerns the way the world is.
- Pluralism holds that the way the world is, is relative to a scheme.
- So pluralism must hold that truth is relative to a scheme.

The first premise of this argument is undoubtedly true, as my discussion in the last few sections, I hope, shows. The second premise, under the reasonable assumption that facts are simply ways the world is, is also true. Pluralism entails a relativity of fact. But what follows from these premises? From the premise that every fact is relative it follows that every true proposition is also relative. This is the connection between fact and content relativity noted in chapter 1. To put it another way, metaphysical pluralism entails that every truth is relative to a conceptual scheme, and if we say that "truth" or "the truth" is a name for all the truths—all the true propositions, in other words—then we can affirm the conclusion of the argument: truth is relative to a scheme. This is what I meant by saying that there was another, trivial interpretation of "truth is relative" that doesn't add anything to metaphysical pluralism.

But here is the important point. Just because every *truth* is relative to a scheme, this does not imply that our *concept* of truth is "truth-for-C."

All truths are relative, yes, but our concept of truth needn't be a relative concept.[23]

There is an entirely general point to be made here. By reasoning similar to what we have been discussing, it might be thought that the pluralist must hold that every concept is relative. But this is a misunderstanding. According to pluralism, every proposition is relative, but not every concept. A proposition is relative when it is determinate only in virtue of its connection to something else. In this book I have taken propositions, true or false, to be relative to conceptual schemes, and I have suggested that this can be understood as saying that the proposition contains an implicit reference to a scheme. On the other hand, a concept is relative when it is determinate or complete only in virtue of its relation to something else. Consider an obviously relative concept, *being to the left of.* Even to understand what I am saying when I say that x is to the left, you must ask, "to the left of what?" Talk of being to the left is always to be understood as being to the left of some y. A relative concept, then, like the relative concept of truth, is a concept that is relative by its very nature *as that concept.*

I think that our minimal notion of truth is not a relative concept, even while, as a relativistic Kantian, I believe that the propositions to which it applies are relative. This sounds odd, but such concepts are not without precedent. It can help to consider some analogous cases. Two good examples are the concepts of spatial coincidence and simultaneity. Minimally speaking, to say that two events are simultaneous is just to say that they happened at the same time. Our ordinary minimal concept of occurring at the same time is not metaphysically loaded. We use it everyday with nary a thought about ultimate reality. "He shot the ball just as the buzzer sounded," we insist, not knowing or caring that, as Einstein showed, there is no absolute fact of the matter. According to the special theory of relativity, whether x and y occur at the same time is always relative to a particular state of uniform motion. All facts about simultaneity are relative facts.[24] But certainly our ordinary, minimal concept of occurring at the same time is not a relative concept. We can employ the concept of simultaneity well before (or even if we never) learn about Einstein's discoveries. The same story holds with our concept of two events happening at the same place. Again, our minimal everyday concept of spatial coincidence is familiar well before we encounter the idea, again due to the special theory, that whether two events occur at the same place is always relative to the state of an observer. Again, the facts are relative, but our minimal, everyday concept is not.

In the same way, one can hold that all propositions are relative to a conceptual scheme, including, of course, all propositions about propositions, without thereby holding that our concepts of truth or proposition are relative concepts. In the same sense in which we understand that x happens at the same time as y is a fact only relative to some state of uniform motion, so the fact that *the proposition that snow is white is true* is relative to some conceptual scheme. But the pluralist needn't hold that this is so *in virtue of the concept of truth*, anymore than we take it that facts about simultaneity are relative in virtue of the concept of simultaneity. The pluralist *already* has an explanation for why the claim that it is true that snow is white is relative: it is a consequence of her general *metaphysical* thesis that every claim is relative to a conceptual scheme.

According to the type of pluralism I've been defending in this book, the conditions under which a proposition is true are determined by the conceptual scheme in which the proposition is expressed. But what makes a proposition true is not its relation to the scheme but whether or not the conditions in question obtain. For a claim to be true (or false), the conditions must be relative to a scheme. Yet the truth of a proposition need not *consist* in its being relative to a scheme. Minimally speaking, the reason that a claim is true is not because it is relative to a scheme (as the truth relativist must hold); it is true because *it is the case*.[25]

For the same reasons, the pluralist is not committed to holding that fact relativism is a consequence of our minimal concept of a fact. A fact, in the minimal sense, is simply what is the case. Now according to metaphysical pluralism, facts are relative, for any state of affairs, obtaining or not, is relative to a scheme. But again, the pluralist needn't hold that it is part of our concept of facts that a scheme-relative state of affairs obtains simply because that state of affairs is relative to a scheme. Its obtaining consists in its being the case.

Our minimal concepts of truth and fact *are* minimal in that they float free of metaphysical debates, including debates between relativism and absolutism. After all, most of our day-to-day thought about the world is not concerned with matters of deep metaphysics. Of course, in advocating that we must conceive of facts as relative to conceptual schemes, pluralism might be taken as *extending* our minimal conceptions of truth and fact in relativist directions. But this does not mean that we should or even can (in a practical sense of "can") let go of our minimal concepts of fact, truth, and proposition. Minimal concepts are the stepladder to metaphysics.

6

The True and the Real

Though we cannot *know* these objects as things in themselves, we must yet be in position at least to *think* them as things in themselves; otherwise we should be landed in the absurd conclusion that there can be appearance without anything that appears.

Immanuel Kant

6.1   Relativism, Inconsistency, and Self-Reference

With the completion of the last chapter, I have addressed the main problem of the book: metaphysical pluralism is compatible with realism about truth. Yet some loose ends, questions, and objections need resolution if the conjunction of MR and pluralism—what I called *relativistic Kantianism*—is to make the sense I claim that it does. The point of this chapter is to confront the most pressing of these concerns. In effect, this means that the last chapter has a slightly different emphasis than the rest of the book. It amounts to defending relativistic Kantianism as a coherent philosophical alternative.

The first issue concerns self-reference. An example of a self-referring claim is "Every sentence is in a language"—including *that* sentence, of course. Such statements must apply to themselves if they are true. Similarly, content relativism states that propositions are relative to conceptual schemes. Presumably, this applies to pluralism itself, including the proposition that every proposition is relative to a conceptual scheme.[1] Some may think that this aspect of pluralism undermines the entire position. If content relativism itself is relative to a conceptual scheme, then there could be a scheme where it is not relative. If so, then pluralism is false, since some propositions would then not be relative to conceptual schemes. On the other hand, if the statement of content relativism were exempt from being relative, again there would be propositions that were not relative to conceptual schemes, and content relativism would be false. Either way, the objection runs, pluralism must be false.

This is a familiar quandary for any type of relativism. The answer to it in this case lies with the distinction between absolute facts and propositions on the one hand and *virtually* absolute facts and propositions on the other. An absolute fact is a state of affairs that obtains independently of any conceptual scheme. Pluralism is committed to denying that there are any such facts. The same story obviously holds with absolute propositions—propositions that are determinate independently of any scheme. This is familiar. But it is rarely, if ever, noticed that metaphysical pluralism is consistent with there being some *virtual absolutes*—facts that do not obtain independently of conceptual schemes but that *do obtain within every scheme*. Pluralism is similarly consistent with virtually absolute propositions, or propositions that are relative to every scheme.

Armed with this distinction, we can now interpret fact and content relativity in a way that avoids the above dilemma.[2] To say that facts are relative is to say that every fact is a relative fact; to say that propositions are relative is to say that every proposition is a relative proposition. This includes these propositions themselves. But this does not imply that some schemes have absolute propositions. It is consistent with content relativism that the statement of it be a virtual absolute—a proposition that is relative to every conceptual scheme.

Several points about virtual absolutes need to be stressed. To begin with, the existence of facts that can be called "virtual" absolutes (as opposed to "real" absolutes) is compatible with the bedrock pluralist view that all thought and language is mediated by one's conceptual scheme. To accept virtual absolutes is not to admit that some propositions are independent of every scheme. Absolutists see no reason to appeal to conceptual schemes in order to understand propositions or facts. On their view, propositions and facts are independent or external to conceptual schemes—every conceptual scheme. So virtual absolutes are not real absolutes.

On the other hand, virtual absolutes require some concepts to figure within every conceptual scheme whatsoever. This is something that the absolutist will believe as well. But the debate between the absolutist and the pluralist on this point reappears at the metalevel. This plays out in several ways.

First, there is the debate over how to regard the concepts in question. The absolutist believes that concepts are determinate (even if our uses of them are not), while the pluralist takes concepts to be fluid, capable of shifting and changing. For example, the pluralist can admit that every scheme must have the minimal concept of an object (what exists, roughly), even while this bare-bones functional concept will be extended in radically different directions from one scheme to another. Thus, while pluralism allows for some virtual absolutes, it implies that many propositions are not relative to every scheme. And incompatible propositions of this sort (propositions that would be inconsistent were they relative to the same scheme) can all be true.

Second, even basic concepts, on the pluralist model of conceptual schemes, are only *contextually* basic (section 2.4). On the pluralist picture, there are no fixed conceptual structures; over time, what is presently fundamental to one's scheme may be pushed to the periphery. In the same sense, to admit that some propositions (basic or not) are now virtually absolute is not to claim that what is relative to every scheme cannot change over time. The pluralist can admit to the possibility of radical conceptual change, even if she cannot imagine how that change would occur.

Third, the pluralist's fluid conception of concepts implies that how one counts propositions is itself a relative matter (sections 3.3, 4.3). According to the pluralist, there are no absolute, scheme-independent facts about whether, for instance, one and the same proposition is relative to several schemes. Whether a proposition is relative to every scheme is not an absolute fact about that proposition. This means that when I say that some proposition is a virtual absolute, I am making a claim within a conceptual scheme.

An analogy may help. Consider a form of fallibilism in epistemology. On this view and common sense alike, I can claim to know something and yet, being conscious of my fallibilist principles, admit that there is a possibility of my being wrong. For instance, I know that there is a tree in the yard. Yet I also know that any belief I have, including any justified belief I have, may be mistaken. I have no actual reason to think that I am mistaken about this particular belief, but as a general principle, I take it that any belief could be mistaken. In the same way, I can claim that some proposition is relative to every conceptual scheme and yet also hold, as a matter of general principle, that I may be wrong about the matter. Given that any claim that I make is internal to my conceptual scheme, the claim that pluralism is relative to every scheme may be relative to my scheme alone. I can allow for this *possibility* even as I claim that as a matter of fact, pluralism is relative to every conceptual scheme.

So the difference between absolutism and pluralism isn't over whether there can be concepts that help compose every scheme and propositions that are relative to every scheme. Both can agree to that. The difference is over the nature of these concepts, propositions, and the facts they reflect. For the absolutist, there is one true conceptual structure that represents the world as it is in itself; for the pluralist, we can use more than one scheme of concepts to truly see the world.

The distinction between virtual absolutes and real absolutes allows the pluralist to avoid the dilemma above. But content and fact relativity would seem to be vulnerable to a related problem: an infinite regress. Again, the problem would seem to arise from the self-referring nature of the pluralist view; content relativity is the idea that every proposition is a relative proposition, including of course, this proposition. Thus the proposition that *propositions are relative* is relative to some conceptual scheme. And so is this last proposition. And so on. It may appear that any attempt to state content relativism is impossible, since any statement of it would result in an infinite regress.

There is a regress here, all right, but not every regress is vicious. To begin with, the schemes to which the iterated proposition is relative may be the same schemes to which the uniterated proposition is relative. Once we remind ourselves of this fact, the threat of the regress in question becomes no more frightening than the regress entailed by the obvious truism that every sentence is in some language. Including *that* sentence, of course. To use another example, consider that for every proposition, if p, then the proposition that p is true. Thus, asserting the proposition that snow is white entails that the proposition that snow is white is true, which in turn entails that the proposition that *the proposition that snow is white is true* is true and so on. *Any* statement thus entails an infinite regress of sorts. But notice that we have absolutely no inclination to view this as problematic. We take it for granted that the multiple occurrences of "true" cancel out, so to speak: the truth value of every statement in the chain is determined simultaneously. This is not a vicious regress, and neither is the regress implied by content relativism. Every proposition, including this one, is relative to one or more schemes. The fact that infinite semantic ascent is possible is no reason for thinking it is problematic.

Furthermore, we need to keep the following in mind: when the pluralist states her view, what she is saying is itself scheme-relative, but when she states her view, she is stating her view—she is not stating that her view is relative to a scheme. Stating a logical consequence of a proposition and stating the proposition itself are two different things. It is a consequence of my stating a proposition that I am committed to that proposition's being true, but to state that snow is white is not identical to stating that it is true that snow is white. In the same sense, to state a proposition, according to pluralism, implies that the proposition is relative to a scheme, but this does not mean that the proposition is identical to the proposition that the proposition is relative to a scheme.

6.2   On Stepping Outside of My Own Skin

It is a consequence of pluralism that we cannot step outside of our skins and compare our thoughts to the world as it is in itself. For the pluralist, there is no one way the world is; the world has no unique structure independent of our conceptual schemes. Thus pluralism is in conflict with the view that our thought must correspond with such a structure to be true. It is sometimes believed to follow from this fact that we can only compare our thoughts to other thoughts. If this were so, pluralism would seem to make an odd partner with any sort of realism, even minimal realism. According to minimal realism, a proposition is true when what it says to be the case is the case. And in many cases, what a proposition says to be the case, what is on the right side of the T-schema in other words, is a state of affairs in the world, not a thought of any sort. In short, MR implies that our thought is about a world outside itself, and yet metaphysical pluralism may seem to deny this possibility.

The mistake here is made when we infer that we can only compare our thoughts with other thoughts from the premise that we cannot compare our thought to the world in itself. Regrettably, this very inference has been made by many a pluralist. For instance, Richard Rorty has cited the following passage of Putnam's as an example of a point on which he "wholeheartedly concurs with Putnam":

Elements of what we call "language" or "mind" penetrate so deeply into what we call "reality" that the very project of representing ourselves as being "mappers of something language-independent" is fatally compromised from the start.[3]

Readers of Rorty know that he is prone to make similar assertions himself. In *Philosophy and the Mirror of Nature*, he says that his favored view of "epistemological behaviorism"

is merely to say that nothing counts as justification unless by reference to what we already accept, and that there is no way to get outside our beliefs and our language so as to find some test other than coherence. (1979, 178)

The familiar argument presented in these passages (and I might have cited numerous others) moves from a recognition of content and fact relativism to a complete rejection of the idea that our words or thoughts can be compared with anything else. Unfortunately, this way of putting the matter makes Rorty sound like an idealist. That would be a mistake; roughly speaking, Rorty's position is not idealism but antirepresentationalism. His basic argument seems to be the following: (a) The very notion of representation—the idea that our thought is representational—is historically linked to the idea that it can represent what is *outside* our language and thought. But (b) since the idea of such representation is incoherent, we can either embrace idealism or simply give up on the idea that thought and language are representational at all. Since classical idealism is presumably not an option for Rorty, he concludes that the pluralist must abandon the notion of "representation" itself (Rorty 1992, 417).

If Rorty is right and the pluralist must deny that there is a representational character to our thought and language, then pluralism is incompatible with any theory of truth other than an explicitly epistemic one, and there is no such position as relativistic Kantianism. If our language or thought is not about a world (even, as Berkeley thought, a "mental world"), then it can't be the case that the features of that world determine whether our statements are true or false. And, of course, minimal realism does imply that it is the world that determines the truth or falsity of our statements. According to MR, it is snow's being white that makes the statement that snow is white true. Even the minimalist way of reading the T-schema requires the concept of representation. Minimal realism about truth is thus incompatible with the view that it is impossible for language or thought to represent a world outside language or thought.

There is no reason to take pluralism as denying the representational character of our thought and language. This has in fact recently been emphasized by Putnam himself: "I agree with Rorty that we have no access to 'unconceptualized reality.' . . . But it doesn't follow that language and thought do not describe something outside themselves, even if that something can only be described by describing it (that is by employing language and thought)" (1994a, 297). According to content relativity, the fact that there is a tree in the yard is relative to a conceptual scheme. But what we say is also relative to a conceptual scheme, and from the conjunction of these two ideas it is natural to infer that what makes it true that there is a tree in the yard (relative to C) is that there is a tree in the yard (relative to C). Pluralists can accept that our language and thought are about things, and I believe that if they are to make their view plausible at all, they must accept it. To say that reality is relative to our conceptual schemes is not to deny that there is any reality; it is to deny that we can describe how it is independent of our conceptualizations. I might put the point this way: the pluralist isn't denying that the mind represents; she is exploring the limits of representation itself.

6.3   Evaluating Schemes

A related question concerns how one can evaluate schemes on the pluralist view, either one's own or someone else's. Again, relativistic Kantianism requires that all cognition is done within a conceptual scheme. Therefore, even if (as I just claimed) pluralism allows that our thoughts represent a world beyond thought, how can I objectively evaluate another scheme if I am always presupposing my own scheme?

This is not a worry for all forms of pluralism. A *weak modal pluralist*, for instance, believes that conceptual schemes other than his own (which he presumes to be yours and mine as well) are possible only in the logical sense. They are physically impossible. On such a view, the question of how one might evaluate conceptual schemes, practically speaking, is moot: there are no other schemes to evaluate. Such conservatism has its merits—it does allow the pluralist to effectively duck some sticky questions while still denying absolutism—but it also seems unmotivated. After all, if one did not believe that divergent conceptual schemes are possible in this world (or worlds with physical laws like those of the actual world), then on what basis would one be a pluralist?

The question of evaluation is also moot when the scheme in question is *totally* alien to one's own. If another's concepts are radically different, then mere comprehension, let alone evaluation, will be impossible. Evaluation of another's scheme requires some common ground, some shared concepts. And the sharing or overlapping of concepts *is* possible, as I've repeatedly argued throughout. One can share a *minimal concept of F* with another even as you employ a more robust extension of that concept. By standing on the common ground of minimal concepts, I may begin to learn more about the culture you live in, your language, your customs, your beliefs, your philosophy—in short, what I called your worldview. Straddling both schemes allows me to assess each. As a result, judging from the basis of our shared concepts, I may find that your views are mistaken, even internal to your own scheme. Or it may be that my perspective is in need of critique. For in addition to assessing the worldviews of others, we must also evaluate our *own* worldview. Or yet again, I may find that, as with Smith's and Johnson's imaginary debate over the contents of the bag, both worldviews express truths, if incompatible ones.

So the fact that worldviews and conceptual schemes can overlap allows for mutual understanding and evaluation. But the latter two possibilities raise a further question: How can I evaluate my *own* worldview objectively if I am presupposing it while doing so? If I cannot escape my worldview, how do I assess it (either by itself or in comparison with another) without engaging in circular reasoning?

What we most often evaluate, of course, is our beliefs. And I can uncontroversially assess the warrant I have for most of my beliefs just so long as I am not assuming those beliefs to be true while doing so. In the same way, I can evaluate many of my concepts and ways of thinking about the world without having to presuppose or use those exact concepts. Circularity becomes a problem only when the beliefs and concepts in question are so *basic* that it is difficult to engage in any thought whatsoever without somehow presupposing those beliefs and concepts.

This problem—the problem of how to evaluate the most basic elements of our thought—is a problem not just for the pluralist. But reflecting on it helps illuminate the pluralist view.

Of course, one can *describe* one's beliefs, concepts, and attitudes while maintaining them. And descriptions can bring out inconsistencies and incoherence. Thus I may examine my basic concepts and find them lacking on these grounds and yet not presuppose those concepts, in any obviously pernicious way, while doing so. On the other hand, there are clearly times when we wish to do more than "conceptual geography." We judge our concepts normatively: as sensible or nonsensical, moral or immoral. This is possible because even while one cannot step outside of all concepts altogether, it is possible to step outside (even if just momentarily) of the conceptual scheme of your immediate community. This is what we might call assuming a *critical standpoint toward a scheme*.[4] Taking a critical standpoint, in the sense I mean it here, is needed when normatively judging one's own scheme. To do so, we must, if only hypothetically, extend our conceptual perspective. This requires adopting concepts that, while minimally connected to our old ways of thinking, are substantial enrichments of those ways of thinking as well. By imagining how we might extend our rusty old concepts in radical new directions, artists, writers, scientists, poets, and metaphysicians are able to get us to see the faults of our current worldview. They supply us with hypothetical vantage points from which to look at ourselves. And it is precisely because they are imagining an extension of our *concepts*, and not just our beliefs, that we are often left confused and uncomprehending in their wake.

The critical standpoint I speak of does not assume absolutism. It is always a standpoint "relative to," and as this implies, there can be no comparing a conceptual structure with the one true conceptual scheme, which captures the way the world is in itself. So the extent to which one can transcend worldviews and their connected conceptual schemes is always limited. But this hardly undermines our ability to engage in constructive and revisionary evaluation of ourselves and others. The point can be seen by attending to the details of evaluation of a more familiar sort. In daily life, the charge that someone cannot be a fit judge on some matter because his relevant views are shot through with prejudice must be taken seriously. But as in the case of metaphysics, it can only be taken seriously so far. There comes a point where we are unable to eliminate all prejudice of a conceptual and emotional sort. Too much of what we are is wrapped within our worldview, and it is a truism that I am in part a product of my formal and cultural education, cognitive capacities, and general historical background. But *merely having a background* cannot prohibit one from making justified appraisals of oneself or others. The extent to which it does is the extent to which no appraisals can be made at all. What matters is whether the sort of background you have is prejudicial *in the particular case at hand*. In the same sense, *merely having a conceptual scheme* cannot prohibit one from making justified appraisals of it or some other scheme. The extent to which possessing a scheme does prevent justified evaluation is the extent to which no evaluation or even comprehension is possible. The pluralist is therefore no worse off with regard to evaluation than any of us are in the judgments that we make in the course of our lives.

The pluralist, then, needn't admit that every possible worldview or conceptual scheme is as good as every other. There are *viable* and *nonviable* worldviews. A viable worldview hangs together, is free from massive internal inconsistency, fits the empirical data, is mostly truthful, and so on. A nonviable worldview is fragmented and inconsistent, ignores the data, and is more often mistaken than not. Of course, there is no calculus to tell us when we have a viable or nonviable scheme. Any judgment about viability will be made with one's own standards. Yet as I just argued, this fact can't be said to prevent us from making judgments. We can only do the best we can, with the standards we have, hoping to make them better as we move along in life.

6.4   Facing the Noumena

Metaphysical pluralism, despite (or because of) all of its argumentative twists and rhetorical turns, can leave us feeling dizzy—as if we were tottering on the edge of a great abyss. We feel the ground slipping away again into paradox. A main reason for this is that the very idea of the relativity of facts generates a version of what Horgan has called the "Kantian dilemma" (1991, 313). Commenting on Putnam's assertion that metaphorically speaking, his view is that "the mind and the world jointly make up the mind and the world" (1981, v), Horgan writes,

> But Putnam's description of his position seems unintelligible even at the metaphorical level, because the metaphors only pose again the question of how anything mind-dependent could ever exist unless sonething mind-independent also existed. How could the mind and the world create themselves, if both are genuinely mind-dependent? Wouldn't a mind dependent Universe require for its existence an already existing, metaphysically real MIND, such as a Berkeleyan MIND or a divine MIND? (1991, 314)

Of course, I've already argued (section 4.4) that the debate between pluralism and absolutism can't be reduced to a debate over dependence or independence of mind. The issue is not mind dependence but relativism. Nonetheless, Horgan's worry cuts as deep when applied to the pluralism I've developed here, as it does when applied to Putnam's view. Essentially, the problem is this. How can it all be relative unless there is a ground for that relativity? In other words, doesn't the relativity of everything require something to be *nonrelative,* something that is independent of our schemes and conceptualizations, something that conceptual schemes are ultimately schemes *of*? I think it does. In section 4.3, I claimed, against Goodman, that the pluralist must hold that our conceptual schemes represent a shared reality. My argument was based in part on the fact that our minimal, basic concept of reality is of a world that impinges on all of us. The concept of a shared reality is deeply presupposed by our worldview.

But this still leaves open the question of what this shared reality is like. As Horgan dryly comments, pluralists typically react to this challenge by adopting a head-in-the-sand or "What, me worry?" rhetorical posture. One can see why shrugging the problem off would be tempting. For it seems that admitting the existence of a single world that schemes represent admits that there is a world that is THE WORLD, that is independent of conceptual schemes. But to do this would seem to create even bigger problems for pluralism—problems that can appear fearsome enough to make anyone want to run for the sand and start digging. For suppose we grant that there is such a thing as THE WORLD—a noumenal realm, as it were. Now either there is a way that world is or there isn't. If there is a way the world is independently of our conceptual schemes, then absolutism is true and pluralism is false. On the other hand, if the world has no way it is in itself, then it does: *the way the world is in itself is that there is no way the world is in itself.* Therefore, a world that is nothing in itself is incoherent. Either way, absolutism appears to triumph. No wonder the pluralist finds it easier to brush the problem off.

The relativistic Kantian can and should admit the obvious truth that there is a single world represented by our conceptual schemes. As I said, we actually do have such a concept, and it is a concept with a use. But its use, I shall argue, is easily misunderstood. Our concept of a single shared reality is neither a concept of a world with a unique structure, as the absolutist believes, nor the concept of a "noumenal realm" that lies beyond the shadows of appearance. Our basic concept of the world is of nothing more or less than the world we live in.

I'll begin my argument in earnest by noting something that Putnam says about Kant:

[According to Kant] the notion of a noumenal world is a kind of limit thought (*Grenz-Begriff*) rather than a clear concept. Today the notion of an noumenal world is perceived as an unnecessary metaphysical element in Kant's thought. (But perhaps Kant is right: perhaps we can't help thinking that there is somehow a mind-independent "ground" for our experiences even if attempts to talk about it lead at once to nonsense.) (1981, 62)

In effect, I believe that Kant *is* right. We have, and must have, a conception of a single world that our conceptual schemes represent. To see this, it is helpful to consider briefly some of Kant's views in a bit more depth. According to the traditional interpretation, Kant believed that there are two worlds: the world of appearances and the noumenal world. On this reading, Kant's view is that our knowledge is only of the world of appearances; our knowledge never penetrates into the "real" or noumenal world—the world-as-it-is-in-itself. This noumenal realm is truly a separate realm of being, one that we can know nothing about. The "two-world" interpretation makes Kant, therefore, into a kind of skeptic: the real world eludes the grasp of our knowledge.

But another interpretation of Kant, made forcefully in recent years by Henry Allison, points in a very different direction. On this view, Kant's distinction between appearances and the thing in itself is actually to be understood as between "a *consideration* of a thing as it appears and a *consideration* of the same thing as it is in itself" (Allison 1983, 241). The difference is not between worlds but between ways of considering one world. On this picture, Kant is saying not that there is a noumenal WORLD, which we cannot know, but that we cannot consider our own world noumenally. Yet as Allison notes, Kant can consistently hold that "although we cannot know [consider] things as they are in themselves, we can nonetheless know how they must be conceived in transcendental reflection" (1983, 241).

To engage in *transcendental* reflection, on Kant's view, is to ascertain a priori the conditions for all possible experience. One of these conditions that transcendental reflection reveals is that we must conceive of there being a ground of our experience and conceptualization. This is presumably Kant's point when (as in the passage quoted at the beginning of this chapter) he says we must be in position at least to *think* of the world or objects as things in themselves (1781/1787, B xxvii). Yet any attempt to conceive of that ground noumenally, or as it is in itself, is impossible. He therefore concludes that what that experience is ultimately *experience of* can only be described as "something in general = x" (as he sometimes says) or as "the transcendental object" (see Kant 1781, A 109, and Allison 1983, 250).

Unfortunately, talk of a transcendental OBJECT makes it sound as if the two-worlds interpretation is right after all. For it seems to suggest that there are two types of objects: the transcendental or noumenal OBJECT and our more homespun phenomenal object. But Allison's interpretation encourages a different reading. Allison's view, again, is that Kant is contrasting not *worlds* (or worlds of objects) but ways of conceptualizing our single shared reality. So even Kant's mention of a transcendental object needn't be understood as a reference to a distinct transcendental

realm. Rather, Kant's position would seem to be that when we are considering our conceptual scheme transcendentally, our concept of the world
is, as Putnam said, a "limit concept." As Allison remarks, this concept
functions very much like a "transcendental pointer" that points not at a
different but invisible world but at one of the conditions for experience.
It brings to our attention the fact that our experience, while always a
function of the conditions of the human mind, is not necessarily *about*
the mind (1983, 244).

Of course, interpreting Kant is a difficult and dark business, and I am
certainly not going to make any confident assertions about what Kant
means. Yet Allison's interpretation of Kant suggests the sort of stance
toward our notion of shared reality that I think the relativistic Kantian
should adopt. Like Kant himself, the relativistic Kantian is essentially
engaging in transcendental reflection; she is reflecting on the metaphysical
conditions under which thought and talk is possible. And like Kant himself, the relativistic Kantian is not contrasting worlds but ways of *conceiv-
ing our one shared reality*. Her view is that we can conceive of the world
not absolutely but only as relative to some conceptual scheme or other.
And it turns out that it is an essential part of any scheme that we have
a concept of a single world that our schemes represent. This is how we
must see ourselves: as part of a reality that is bigger than us and yet
limited by us at the very same time.

Part of the reason we have a difficult time accepting this way of looking
at the matter is the dualism that lurks within the very language of
"scheme" and "world." Schemes and perspectives must be schemes and
perspectives of something, and if we cannot step outside all perspectives
to see that something, this something transforms in our minds into a mere
"something in general = *x*." *But surely it is the gravest of mistakes to
take these perspectival metaphors too literally.* When we speak of "the
world," we are not speaking of a distinct entity—a distant country dimly
glimpsed through the mists of language. To think that our concept of the
world in general is the concept of a VERY BIG THING is to misunderstand
it and miss its purpose. The "real world" cannot be a distinct thing, because *we are in that world*. Put simply, our minimal concept of the world
is just the notion of everything, and our concept of *everything* is not the
concept of one distinct thing among others. The purpose of such a con-

cept is not to refer to an object but to act as a transcendental pointer toward the conditions of our thought.

In sum, my suggestion is that a single, shared, "real" world is clearly impossible if what we mean by "the real world" is a realm of being literally beyond ourselves—separate from us and our concepts. Such a concept of noumenal reality is incoherent. But the concept *is* coherent if we mean by the term ourselves and all other things. Philosophically speaking, to note that the real world exists in this second sense is necessary but ultimately trivial. It can amount to nothing more than the linguistic analogue of the expansive gesture one might make when asked what exists. "All this," we might say, opening our arms to everything. And we would be right. A concept of the real or ultimate world is therefore not to be feared by the pluralist. It serves no other function but to remind us that our world is *the* world, after all.

6.5   The Purpose of Metaphysics

Despite my occasional remarks to the contrary, pluralism may seem to make substantive metaphysical inquiry impossible. As John Post puts it, "the complaint is not that pluralism bakes no bread but that it paints no pictures, builds no worlds" (1987, 307). If pluralists are content merely to point out that there are numerous equally correct perspectives on reality, they run the risk of being perceived as "kibitzing dilettantes" who ignore the "real drama in philosophy . . . , [namely] pairing the rage for order with delight in near chaotic variety" (Post 1987, 307).

I take this worry seriously. Post is surely right that if one looks to metaphysics at all, it is for help in finding wisdom about our world and our place within it. But as Post insinuates, views like metaphysical pluralism are often portrayed (and portray themselves) as antimetaphysical and even antiphilosophical. The point of many pluralist-leaning writers seems to be that once we see that there are many equally correct metaphysical views, we should stop doing metaphysics.

This is not the way I look at the matter. First, the idea that once we accept metaphysical pluralism we should stop doing metaphysics and get on with doing something useful, like (say) science, betrays a lingering allegiance to absolutism. It reveals that one is still caught up in judging an enterprise by its ability to gain absolute access to ultimate truth; if metaphysics has no such access, we must rinse our hands of it. Yet fully embraced, this attitude would quickly lead to a pervasive (and depressing) nihilistic skepticism, not to mention contradiction. If metaphysical pluralism teaches us anything, it is that no one enterprise has sole access to absolute truth—not because many do, but because there is no such thing as absolute truth to begin with.

Second, pluralist philosophies that deny the possibility of metaphysics are built on a lie. Metaphysical pluralism is not just concerned with metaphysics; it is a metaphysics. The relativistic Kantian, in telling us that there is no absolute truth about the nature of reality, is telling us about reality. As I've been insisting throughout the last two sections, to deny that reality is absolute is not to deny reality.

Metaphysics, on this picture, is the investigation of the presuppositions—as Collingwood would have called them—of one's contextual situation. The contextually basic concepts of one's conceptual scheme are the tools and the subject alike of the metaphysician. These concepts are *contextually* basic, because they too can shift and change; unlike Kant, or even Strawson, the pluralist takes every concept to have a history.

This way of putting the matter makes it sound as if metaphysical "investigation" is really just the description of our conceptual scheme. Ontology becomes what Strawson called "descriptive metaphysics," according to which metaphysicians describe our way of thinking about the world by mapping our conceptual geography. Metaphysics, on this view, is a cousin of conceptual analysis, differing only in "scope and generality" (Strawson 1959, xiii).

Conceptual description is an important part of metaphysical inquiry. But it is not the only part. Metaphysics isn't always descriptive, and even when it is descriptive, it isn't always descriptive of the conceptual landscape.

Consider a painting—Van Gogh's *Wheat Field with Crows*, for example. Is *Wheat Field with Crows* a description, a representation of something? Undoubtedly; it depicts a wheat field with crows flying above it. But is that all it is? Undoubtedly not. It is also a reflection on our thought about things like crows, on how we see them, and on how we might see them at those times when we filter life through a darker emotional lens.

Paintings, especially very good paintings, are representations at once of the world *and* of one's thought about that world. For the painter, these are not separated into distinct projects. Representing the world and representing thought and feelings about that world are simply two aspects of painting itself. The same is true for metaphysics. Metaphysicians describe our world, yes, but in doing so, metaphysics is at the same time a description of how the world *presents itself to us*. We can separate these projects in theory, but in practice the two intertwine.

Metaphysics, as Strawson knew, can also be revisionary: it can change how we think about ourselves and the universe. But for Strawson, revisionary metaphysics was always at the service of descriptive metaphysics (1959, xiii). This may sometimes be true, for it is difficult to change one's worldview—or at least to change it for the better—unless one knows how it presently is. Yet I think it more likely that any metaphysical project has both revisionary and descriptive aspects. It is difficult to avoid changing one's worldview even as you bring to light its fundamental elements.

My own bias is toward the revisionary aspect of metaphysical inquiry. Again, it strikes me that a comparison with art is useful. Emerson noted that "the use of literature is to afford us a platform whence we may command a view of our present life, a purchase by which we may move it" (1883, 29). This applies to philosophical literature just as well as it does to poetry. There would be little point to deep metaphysical investigation if it could not move us to think and act differently. Metaphysics seeks not just the truth but a truth that moves.

The revision of our worldview and conceptual schemes is accomplished by the extension of our basic and minimal concepts. Even as the dualist philosopher describes the mind as a nonphysical substance, she is extending our shared minimal concept of mind, and hence pulling our conceptual scheme in a new direction. Pluralism, and certainly the form of pluralism I discuss in this essay, is as revisionary as it is descriptive. In telling us that the world is many and not one, the pluralist too is extending our minimal concepts. The result is that pluralism doesn't call for an end to pictures. It paints us another.

Notes

Introduction

1. See Putnam's Dewey Lectures (1994b).

2. This distinction is due to Price 1992, 389–390.

3. Nonreductivist theories of mind are familiar. See for example, Davidson 1980, Van Gulick 1992, and Horgan 1994. John Post (1987) is perhaps the most systematic defender of radical vertical pluralism, which he quite rightly takes to be consistent with realism about truth.

Chapter 1

1. Among the many important philosophers who believe in a global materialism of this sort are Michael Devitt (1984, 23) and David Lewis (1983, xi).

2. Chris Swoyer makes the same point in his brief but lucid discussion of these issues (1982, 86 ff).

3. In this century, philosophers who have accepted this general constructivist epistemology have extended it to cover raw sensory data as well. Hence, Hilary Putnam, writing as a pluralist, denies "that there are any inputs which are not themselves to some extent shaped by our concepts" (1981, 54). Even the raw sensory Given in experience is seen by Putnam as infiltrated by our concepts.

4. Rorty 1979, 176. Goodman 1978, 120. Putnam, 1981, 121, 49–50; also 1990, 27–29. Recently Putnam seems to de-emphasize the epistemic nature of his account of truth (see lecture 3 of his Dewey Lectures [1994b] and "The Question of Realism" in 1994a).

5. See McMichael 1988, Lepore and Loewer 1988, and Devitt 1984 for examples.

6. Note that this minimal use of "proposition" is not committed to the thesis that propositions are the meanings of sentences, although it is consistent with that thesis. Indeed, the term "proposition" is often used quite differently by

contemporary philosophers. I am placing as little weight on it as possible. I use "proposition" only as a term of art that conveniently allows me to distinguish *what is said* from the saying of it. This in turn allows me to attribute truth values to what is said or believed, and not the saying or believing. If you have some other favored way of making this distinction (by appealing to statements, for example), then simply replace "proposition" with the less offensive terminology.

7. By "metaphysical necessity" I simply mean the strongest form of necessity possible, whether that be logical, "broadly logical," etc.

8. Of course, absolutists can tolerate uncontentious relativization to individuals of the sort exhibited by statements about an object's color or taste. Furthermore, and as I note below in the text, one needn't be an absolutist about everything.

9. For instance, if absolutism did require that the list of true propositions be complete, then it would be subject to the following paradox: if the one true list of propositions is itself a proposition, it would have to be included in itself. Paul Bloomfield has suggested to me that Gödel's proof of the incompleteness of arithmetic might cause similar problems. But "completeness" in this sense is not *required* by absolutism. All that is required is that, however many propositions there are, their content is absolute. For more on these paradoxes, see Grim 1991 and Putnam 1990, 11–18.

10. Hence I also am indifferent to accounts that distinguish facts from states of affairs (as in Slote 1975, 92–108). Such a distinction is perfectly consistent with absolutism (and pluralism) since presumably either facts and states of affairs will be both absolute and relative at once.

11. For examples of this type and discussions thereof, see Amelie Rorty's 1976 collection.

12. This example is a favorite of Putnam's; see 1989, 110.

13. Goodman 1978, 113–115; Putnam 1992a, 118–119; Putnam 1978, 130–133.

14. Indeed, it would be surprising—and a cause for dismay among some ontologists—if ontological theories, as traditionally conceived, did have an impact on our social or scientific practices. Such results would run counter to Plato's dictum that we must save the appearances.

15. See van Inwagen 1990.

16. The underlying problem here is really the so-called "paradox of analysis," according to which if an analysis contains more information than the term it is meant to analyze, it is false; if the exact amount, trivial. The proper solution, it seems to me, and the one implicitly embraced in the text, is that in expressing a proposition we needn't *mean* to say what we in fact *do* say. That is, our intentions do not determine content.

17. Those interested in problems surrounding self-reference will find them addressed in section 6.1.

18. Some might be tempted to argue that fact relativism entails only the relativity of true propositions. Yet it would surely be ad hoc to stipulate that false proposi-

tions are absolute when true ones are not. More important, if all facts are relative, then for many values of x, we could affirm that it is not a fact that x in C, or alternatively, that it is a fact that it is not the case that x in C. In such cases, there will be the false proposition that x in C. So if facts are universally relative, propositions will be so as well.

19. For instance, Hartry Field has argued that one can believe in a "fixed totality of objects" without believing in one true story of the world (1982, 554–555). Horgan (1991, 300) Sosa (1993a, 608) and Sacks (1989, 41) make similar claims.

20. Not all those whom I would identify as absolutists deny the inference, however. As I read him, Bernard Williams (1985, 138–139) implicitly accepts it, and so, I think, does William Alston (1996, 173–178).

21. One explanation for the necessity of the T-equivalences is that their component propositions are identical in content: "It is true that p" says nothing more than "p". But this deflationary reading is not the only one available, and certainly not needed here. See section 5.5 for more discussion of this point.

22. This is in fact the way Putnam puts the point, since his paradigm of the metaphysical realist is his physicalist and realist former self (see, e.g., 1990, 30–42).

23. See 1981, 49–50; 1990, 27–29.

24. An exception is Alston (1996).

Chapter 2

1. Profitable discussions of the notion include Davidson 1984, Rescher 1980, and Swoyer 1982. Two very recent excellent discussions are Hacker 1996 and Case 1997.

2. James (1907) gets the phrase from Clerk Maxwell, as he notes.

3. Quine's point about his usage of "conceptual scheme" is in his 1981 book, 41. Why he thought that such an esoteric term was a part of "ordinary language," I have no idea.

4. One might wonder what is included within the scope of the quantifier "any" here. In other words, are the categories the categories for all possible *human* experience and knowledge? Or did Kant intend his account to cover any thinker whatsoever, human or not? As William Lawhead has pointed out to me, in the first *Critique* (B71 ff), Kant says that time is not a form of intuition for God and that he is unsure whether it is or is not for other finite creatures. This indicates a willingness to tolerate a limited or weak form of pluralism. Nonetheless, I continue to assume the stronger interpretation, namely that the categories structure experience for any possible cognizer. I think that this is certainly the general drift of Kant's thought, but in the end I won't argue the details. I am more interested in presenting a *Kantian* model of conceptual schemes.

5. On Kant's transcendental psychology, compare Bennett 1966 and Kitcher 1990.

6. By calling the forms of intuition "formal concepts," I don't mean to suggest that Kant thought of space and time as concepts per se, although he clearly thought they functioned in a somewhat similar way. I gloss over these particulars in the text simply because they are unnecessary for my purposes.

7. See Carnap's "Empiricism, Semantics, and Ontology" (1953).

8. That is, the following arguments rely on several highly contentious premises (such as distinction between a sentence and the proposition it expresses), and so I wouldn't expect either Quine or Davidson to be persuaded. But persuading them is not my point; rather, I mean to be pointing out that even if one *rejects* Davidson's argument against QM, there are still good reasons to abandon QM anyway.

9. For a good example of this tendency, see Putnam 1990, 96–103.

10. See, for example, Putnam 1983, 4; 1981, 54–55.

11. This claim is mirrored on the epistemic plain of battle by philosophers like Annis (1978) and Henderson (1994), who discuss a position called contextualism, according to which there can be contextually basic beliefs—beliefs not justified by other beliefs within or relative to a certain context.

12. Rorty (1972) makes this point.

Chapter 3

1. These remarks are meant not as a *theory* of concepts but rather as platitudes that demarcate what I am talking about when I use the word "concept." Like any functional description that explains something in terms of what it does, rather than what it is, these minimal platitudes don't entail a particular ontology. As far as the minimal notion of concepts is concerned, concepts may turn out be mental particulars, computational rules exemplified by our neural architecture, abstract objects, dispositions, or entities reducible to our uses of words. So, for example, while I shall sometimes equate concepts with the meanings of words, this is simply a practical shortcut. The concepts I am concerned with can be expressed verbally, and in these cases, the identification of concepts with word meanings is useful. In short, my minimalist understanding of concepts allows me to examine how concepts must function if they are to play the role the pluralist would ask of them, without getting bogged down in ontological issues.

2. That said, I am sympathetic with Nicholas Wolterstorff's claim that "the fundamental issue in our contemporary debate between realists and anti-realists is the nature of our concepts" (1984, 63). Unlike Wolterstorff, however, I am reluctant to identify any issue in such a wide-ranging debate as *the* issue on which the debate turns.

3. I take this metaphor from Wittgenstein's allusion to his former self's preconceived idea of the "crystalline purity" of language (1958, sec. 108).

4. For an excellent resource for more information on these distinctions, and on Waismann's contributions, see Baker and Hacker, 1980a, 209–228.

5. The following discussion draws heavily from Baker and Hacker 1980a, 185–208.

6. I refer to Putnam's classic article "The Meaning of 'Meaning'" (1975).

7. It was included as an "exhibition sport" in the 1996 Atlanta games.

8. Alternatively, however, one might say that we share many different but overlapping concepts of a game. I will use "one fluid concept" and "many distinct but overlapping concepts" interchangeably.

9. I am, of course, ignoring problems raised by Gettier (1963), problems to the effect that justified true belief is not sufficient for knowledge.

10. They are intuitively coherent in the case of the minimal concept of epistemic justification as well, I think. See Moser 1993 and also Alston's 1993 discussion of different concepts of justification. Alston maintains that there isn't even a minimal concept of justification.

11. Fact and content relativism hold at the "meta" level as well as at the "object" level. Propositions about propositions are also relative. An infinite regress looms, but as we shall see in section in 6.1, it is a regress without teeth.

12. Wittgenstein makes this comment in reference to the concept of a person in *The Blue Book* (1960, 62).

Chapter 4

1. For an example of this sort of argument, see McMichael 1988, 67–70.

2. Harré and Krausz (1996, 26–27) pose this question.

3. In all fairness, Searle's point here may be different than Blackburn's. Perhaps Searle is claiming that there is no *absolutely determinate* concept of an object that could be shared by Smith and Johnson (despite their possible beliefs to the contrary). If so, I agree, since I make this point below.

4. The first definition is essentially Frege's view (see Dummett 1981, chap. 4). The second is Quine's more refined gloss on the same idea (see, e.g., Quine, "On What There Is" [1953] and "Speaking of Objects" and "Existence and Quantification" in his 1969 collection).

5. A helpful and interesting recent discussion of these issues can be found in Lowe 1995. See also Williams 1981.

6. Quine 1969, 94.

7. Quine 1980, 13.

8. It is worth noting that the main argument of this section overlaps to some degree with claims made by C. J. F. Williams in his fascinating study *What Is Existence?* (1981), especially chap. 7. Williams approach is more concerned with technical questions in logic than my own, and he does not draw any implications for pluralism from his arguments. Yet the main thesis of the present section, namely that existence has no essence, is clearly in line with Williams's view that "exist" never functions as "a first-level predicate" (1981, 181).

9. José Benardete (1989, 22–23) entertains this position.

10. I refer here to those persuaded by the causal theory of reference, e.g., Devitt (1984).

11. The original statement of this objection can be found in Alston 1958, 18–19. Alston's position is defended by Searle (1969, 103–13). See also the exchange between Searle and Peter van Inwagen on this subject in Lepore and Van Gulick 1991, 345–358 and 386–88.

12. Some pluralists are tempted to go a different way in response to such problems and claim that Smith's and Johnson's sentences are actually ambiguous between assertions of fact and normative proposals about how the *concept of an object should be applied* in the present case. It is these normative proposals, one might suggest, that are truly in conflict. Such a view would be reminiscent of Carnap's work in "Empiricism, Semantics, and Ontology" (1953). From a verificationist outlook like Carnap's, normative evaluations are inherently nonfactual—they cannot be true or false. Hence, while Smith and Johnson are expressing incompatible *attitudes*, they are not, strictly speaking, uttering inconsistent *assertions*, for they are not asserting anything at all! Like many contemporary students of philosophy, I find Carnap's description of debates between Smith and Johnson implausible. For there seems to be no justification, other than allegiance to a radical verificationist semantics and a sharp and unforgiving division between the normative and the factual, for the belief that disputes over the nature of minds or the universe do not involve assertions. Fortunately, the metaphysical pluralist is not pressed to adopt a Carnapian position.

Chapter 5

1. *Metaphysics* 1011b26. Kirkam (1992, 120), for instance, interprets this view as a correspondence theory, as does Tarski (1944).

2. In his more recent work (1994b), Putnam appears to have significantly weakened his commitment to an explicitly epistemic theory of truth. I shall continue to concentrate on his earlier views, however, since it is the epistemic conception that I am interested in here.

3. The word "relevant" is included here for the obvious reason that in order to be in an ideal position to assess the epistemic status of a proposition, one needn't have at one's fingertips all information, including superfluous or trivial information. Of course, as Alston (1996, 197) points out, some restrictions need to be placed on what counts as relevant as well. Clearly, the epistemic theorist can't simply say that one has all the relevant evidence for p when one is in possession of all the truths that bear on p. That would make things a bit too easy.

4. Alcoff (1995) is one writer who is inclined to interpret Putnam explicitly as a coherence theorist.

5. Horgan (1991), also makes this objection.

6. My point here is not based on unflagging allegiance to bivalence. As a pluralist, I have no such allegiance, as chapters 3 and 4 imply. I just don't think that considerations about truth should be all that drives our opinions about what counts as a proposition with indeterminate truth value. Further (and this is my specific point here), there is nothing about propositions like (a) and (b) that should force us to think that they don't or can't have a determinate truth value, even if, like all other truth-values, that value is determinate only relative to a conceptual scheme.

7. For instance, see Williams 1976, Price 1988, and Grover 1992. On the difficulty of formulating *some* types of deflationary theories, see David 1994.

8. For some recent objections, see David 1994, and Kirkham 1992, 321 ff.

9. Steven Rappaport (1993) may be an exception. See note 23 below.

10. There has been some tendency (though not by Quine, I think) to confuse Tarski's Convention T, or his "material adequacy" *condition* for theories of truth, with Tarski's own definition of truth. Further, it is fairly clear that Tarski thought of himself as a type of correspondence theorist, even if, as some allege, his theory is not a "real" correspondence theory (see his introductory remarks in his 1944 essay, for instance). Kirkham (1992, 170–172 and 186) is a handy reference for the ins and outs of the scholarly debate on this topic.

11. I am not (here or in the next few pages) actually quantifying over propositions in stating these or similar principles. Like the T-schema, CT* should be taken only as an informal schema, that is, as a recipe for constructing true biconditionals of a certain form. But if you wish, we can generalize or quantify the schema by using substitutional quantification. For example, we could take "p" to range over names of propositions, "q" to range over names of facts, and "R" as replacing "corresponds to." If so, then reading the quantifier substitutionally, we could say the following:

$(p)\{p$ is true iff $(\exists q)[pRq$ & $q]\}$

In other words, the result of replacing "p" with any name of a proposition, "q" with any name of a fact, and "R" with "corresponds to" results in a true biconditional.

12. Again in substitutional-quantification notation:

$(p)\{p$ is true iff $(\exists q)[p = q$ & $q]\}$

13. The matter gets more complicated, however, when one is dealing with more complex (e.g., quantified) sentences.

14. Compare Alston, who claims that all his position requires is a commitment to "the primacy of locutions in which 'true' and 'false' are predicated of what is specified by 'that' clauses and other proposition-specifying clauses" (1996, 21).

15. This is not to be confused with the question of whether MR is consistent with varying accounts of what properties are in general. It surely is, as is any other theory of truth. That is, any theory of truth can hold that properties are universals or sets of scattered particulars, etc.

16. Crispin Wright makes a similar comment: "The [truth] predicate serves to express a basic norm of propositional thought and expression. And once that

much is granted [Horwich's claim about the truth property] looks merely dogmatic: any normative property may or may not allow illuminating analysis—it remains to be argued whether, or why, there is, or is not, scope for further philosophical insight in this case" (1992, 23).

17. One worry is that insofar as she is a minimal realist, a metaphysical pluralist will not be able to adopt as wide a pluralism about truth as Wright is advocating. For one of the platitudes the minimal realist sees in TS itself is that truth is not an epistemic property of any sort. I argue below, however, that MR, suitably understood, is compatible with "indirect" extensions of the concept of truth into "antirealist" discourse.

18. It is worth considering for a moment whether truth could be understood as another type of fluid concept, a family-resemblance concept. One sometimes gets the sense that Wittgenstein thought of the issue in this way (see, for example, 1958, sec. 136–137)—an interpretation that is encouraged when one reads him as a deflationist. A deflationist view, after all, is one according to which none of the propositions that we call "true" share any property in virtue of which they are true. And a concept is a family-resemblance concept, in Wittgenstein's sense, just when the "objects" to which it applies share no unique and common property. So on one reading of the situation, to take a deflationary stand toward truth is just to take it as a family-resemblance concept. Whether or not this is the right way to interpret the suggestion that truth is a family-resemblance concept, it is clear that an adoption of MR blocks this path. For MR does entail that there is something that true propositions have in common: their adherence to TS realistically interpreted.

19. Despite its similarities to the view I'm suggesting, Horgan's view could not ultimately be adopted by the metaphysical pluralist. As the words "strict" and "tight" suggest, Horgan's brand of alethic pluralism is *hierarchical*. For Horgan, there is "one right ontology" (1991, 315–316), which is a type of materialism.

20. "How sharper than a serpent's tooth it is to have a thankless child!"

21. The *most* it would show (and I am not entirely convinced of this) is that there are indeterminate instances of the T-schema and MR. But that should not be alarming, since we've already accepted the existence of indeterminate propositions in the first place. Further, as Kirkham (1992, 177) notes, even if there are indeterminate instances of the T-schema, it will still be the case that no instances of the schema are false.

22. Of course, there is more to be said about vagueness (particularly about indeterminate truth values and their logic) and also more to be said about various technical issues that impinge on any discussion of truth. These include the liar paradox (and its several versions), substitutional quantification, meaning, and the nature of conceptual truth. But discussion of any of these issues would take us far afield from our primary concern with pluralism, and so I will leave them untouched in the present essay.

23. Steven Rappaport (1993) has argued that what he calls "metaphysical relativism" does not entail truth relativism as well. But his argument is markedly

different from mine. According to Rappaport, metaphysical relativism is consistent with the "disquotational" theory of truth, which he claims does not entail that truth is relative. See our exchange on the topic (Lynch 1997, Rappaport 1997).

24. An excellent introduction to these issues is Sklar 1992, especially pp. 25–40.

25. A particularly desperate objection at this point would be to claim " 'Snow is white in C' is true" is just another way of saying that "Snow is white" is true-in-C. Since the pluralist must accept the former sentence (it is just an example of content relativism), the objection claims that she must also accept the latter sentence, which employs a relative concept of truth. Thus pluralism implies truth relativism after all. But the fact (if it is a fact) that the two sentences are synonymous shows nothing. Their mere synonymy tells us nothing about which is the more accurate statement of the point. Further, we needn't agree that the two sentences are synonymous anyway. As I understand it, to relativize the concept of truth is to claim that the meaning of the word "true" is "true for a particular conceptual scheme." But this entails that the meaning of the word "true" changes from scheme to scheme. This is not a consequence of content relativism. Content relativism is consistent with the view that our minimal concept of truth is stable across conceptual schemes. What we relativize makes a difference.

Chapter 6

1. Of course, I am concerned in this book with a metaphysical pluralism that strictly speaking, is about metaphysical facts and propositions only. But this point is irrelevant here. First, as I argued in the Introduction, I think that metaphysical pluralism entails a global pluralism. Second, the problem of self-reference still arises for metaphysical pluralism anyway, since pluralism is obviously a "metaphysical proposition" itself.

2. In an excellent recent article on relativism (1997), Steven D. Hales would appear to make a similar distinction for relativism with regard to the concept of truth.

3. Rorty 1993, 443. The quote comes from Putnam 1990, 28.

4. Conversations with the literary critic Robert Neustadt suggest that assuming the critical standpoint relative to one's own conceptual scheme is similar to what literary and art critics call achieving "critical distance."

References

Alcoff, L. 1996. *Real Knowing: New Versions of the Coherence Theory*. Ithaca: Cornell University Press.

Allison, H. 1983. *Kant's Transcendental Idealism*. New Haven: Yale University Press.

Alston, W. P. 1958. "Ontological Commitment." *Philosophical Studies* 9: 8–17.

Alston, W. P. 1979. "Yes, Virginia, There Is a Real World." *Proceedings of the American Philosophical Association* 52: 779–808.

Alston, W. P. 1993. "Epistemic Desiderata." *Philosophy and Phenomenological Research* 53, no. 3: 528–550.

Alston, W. P. 1996. *A Realist Conception of Truth*. Ithaca: Cornell University Press.

Annis, D. 1978. "A Contextualist Theory of Epistemic Justification." *Philosophical Quarterly* 15: 213–219.

Austin, J. L. 1950. "Truth." Reprinted in Pitcher 1964.

Austin, J. L. 1962. *Sense and Sensibilia*. Oxford: Oxford University Press.

Baker, G. P., and Hacker, P. M. S. 1980a. *Wittgenstein on Meaning and Understanding*. Oxford: Basil Blackwell.

Baker, G. P., and Hacker, P. M. S. 1980b. *An Analytical Commentary on Wittgenstein's Philosophical Investigations*. Oxford: Basil Blackwell.

Benardete, J. 1989. *Metaphysics: The Logical Approach*. Oxford: Oxford University Press.

Bennett, J. 1966. *Kant's Analytic*. Cambridge: Cambridge University Press.

Blackburn, S. 1994. "Enchanting Views." In *Reading Putnam*, edited by P. Clark and B. Hale. Oxford: Cambridge University Press.

Carnap, R. 1953. "Empiricism, Semantics, and Ontology." In *Readings in Philosophy of Science*, edited by P. Weiner. New York: Charles Scribner's Sons.

Case, J. 1997. "On the Right Idea of a Conceptual Scheme." *Southern Journal of Philosophy* 35: 1–18.

Cavell, S. 1969. *Must We Mean What We Say?* New York: Scribner Sons.

Collingwood, R. G. 1940. *An Essay on Metaphysics*. Oxford: Oxford University Press.

David, M. 1994. *Correspondence and Disquotation*. Oxford: Oxford University Press.

Davidson, D. 1980. *Essays on Actions and Events*. Oxford: Oxford University Press.

Davidson, D. 1984. *Inquiries into Truth and Interpretation*. Oxford: Oxford University Press.

Davidson, D. 1990. "The Structure and Content of Truth." *Journal of Philosophy* 87: 279–328.

Devitt, M. 1984. *Realism and Truth*. Princeton: Princeton University Press.

Dummett, M. 1978. *Truth and Other Enigmas*. Cambridge: Harvard University Press.

Dummett, M. 1981. *Frege: Philosophy of Language*. 2nd ed. Cambridge: Harvard University Press.

Emerson, R. W. 1883. "Circles." Reprinted in *Pragmatism: A Contemporary Reader*, edited by R. Goodman. New York: Routledge, 1995.

Field, H. 1972. "Tarksi's Theory of Truth." *Journal of Philosophy* 69: 347–375.

Field, H. 1982. "Realism and Relativism." *Journal of Philosophy* 79: 553–567.

Fogelin, R. 1996. "Wittgenstein's Critique of Philosophy." In *The Cambridge Companion to Wittgenstein*, edited by H. Sluga and D. Stern. Cambridge: Cambridge University Press.

Frege, G. 1892. "On Sense and Reference." In Frege 1952.

Frege, G. 1952. *Translations from the Philosophical Writings of Gottlob Frege*. Edited by P. Geach and M. Black. New York: Philosophical Library.

French, P., Uehling, T., and Wettstein, H., eds. 1988. *Realism and Antirealism*. Midwest Studies in Philosophy, no. 12. Minneapolis: University of Minnesota Press.

Gettier, E. 1963. "Is Justified True Belief Knowledge?" *Analysis* 23: 121–123.

Glock, H. J. 1996. "Necessity and Normativity." In *The Cambridge Companion to Wittgenstein*, edited by H. Sluga and D. Stern. Cambridge: Cambridge University Press.

Goodman, N. 1978. *Ways of Worldmaking*. Indianapolis: Hackett Publishing Co.

Goodman, N. 1984. *Of Mind and Other Matters*. Cambridge: Harvard University Press.

Grim, P. 1991. *The Incomplete Universe*. Cambridge: MIT Press.

Grover, D. 1992. *A Prosentential Theory of Truth*. Princeton: Princeton University Press.

Gupta, A. 1993. "Minimalism." In Tomberlin 1993.

Hacker, P. M. S. 1996. "On Davidson's Idea of a Conceptual Scheme." *Philosophical Quarterly* 46: 289–307.

Haldane, J., and Wright, C., eds. 1993. *Reality, Representation, and Projection.* Oxford: Oxford University Press.

Hales, S. 1997. "A Consistent Relativism." *Mind* 106, no. 421: 33–52.

Harré, R., and Krausz, M. 1996. *Varieties of Relativism.* Oxford: Basil Blackwell.

Hawking, S. 1988. *A Brief History of Time.* New York: Bantam Books.

Heal, J. 1989. *Fact and Meaning: Quine and Wittgenstein on Philosophy of Language.* Oxford: Basil Blackwell.

Heidegger, M. 1993. "The Essence of Truth." In *Martin Heidegger: Basic Writings*, edited by D. Krell. San Fransisco: HarperCollins.

Henderson, D. 1994. "Epistemic Competence and Contextualist Epistemology." *Journal of Philosophy* 91: 627–649.

Hintakka, J. 1989. *Investigating Wittgenstein.* Oxford: Basil Blackwell.

Horgan, T. 1986. "Psychologism, Semantics, and Ontology." *Noûs* 20: 21–31.

Horgan, T. 1991. "Metaphysical Realism and Psychologistic Semantics." *Erkenntnis* 34: 297–322.

Horgan, T. 1994. "Nonreductive Materialism." In *The Mind-Body Problem*, edited by R. Warner and T. Szubka. Oxford: Blackwell.

Horgan, T. 1996. "The Perils of Epistemic Reductionism." *Philosophy and Phenomenological Research* 56, no. 4: 801–807.

Horgan, T., and Tienson, J. 1995. *Connectionism and the Philosophy of Psychology.* Cambridge: MIT Press.

Horkheimer, M. 1995. "On the Problem of Truth." *Between Philosophy and Social Science.* Cambridge: MIT Press.

Horwich, P. 1990. *Truth.* Oxford: Basil Blackwell.

James, W. 1907. *Pragmatism.* Cambridge: Harvard University Press, 1975.

James, W. 1909. *The Meaning of Truth.* Cambridge: Harvard University Press, 1975.

Johnston, M. 1993a. "Objectivity Refigured: Pragmatism without Verificationism." In Haldane and Wright 1993.

Johnston, M. 1993b. "Verificationism as Philosophical Narcissism." In Tomberlin 1993.

Kant, I. 1781. *Critique of Pure Reason.* Translated by N. Kemp Smith. New York: St. Martins, 1965.

Kirkham, R. 1992. *Theories of Truth: A Critical Introduction.* Cambridge: MIT Press.

Kitcher, P. 1990. *Kant's Transcendental Psychology.* Oxford: Oxford University Press.

Kuhn, T. 1962. *The Structure of Scientific Revolutions*. Chicago: University of Chicago Press.

Lepore, E., and Loewer, B. 1988. "A Putnam's Progress." In French, Uehling, and Wettstein 1988.

Lepore, E., and Van Gulick, R., eds. 1991. *John Searle and His Critics*. Oxford: Basil Blackwell.

Lewis, D. 1983. *Philosophical Papers*. Vol. 1. Oxford: Oxford University Press.

Loux, M., ed. 1979. *Readings in the Metaphysics of Modality*. Ithaca: Cornell University Press.

Lowe, E. J. 1995. "The Metaphysics of Abstract Objects." *Journal of Philosophy* 92, no. 1: 509–524.

Lynch, M. 1997. "Relativism and Truth: Reply to Rappaport." *Philosophia* 25: 417–422.

Lynch, M. 1997. "Minimal Realism or Realistic Minimalism?" *Philosophical Quarterly* 47: 512–518.

Lynch, M. 1998. "Three Models of Conceptual Schemes." *Inquiry* 40, no. 4: 407–426.

Margolis, J. 1991. *The Truth about Relativism*. Oxford: Basil Blackwell.

McDowell, J. 1994. *Mind and World*. Cambridge: Harvard University Press.

McMichael, A. 1988. "Creative Ontology and Absolute Truth." In French, Uehling, and Wettstein 1988.

Moser, P. 1993. *Philosophy after Objectivity*. Oxford: Oxford University Press.

Nagel, T. 1974. "What Is It Like to Be a Bat?" *Philosophical Review* 83: 435–450.

Peacocke, C. 1992. *A Study of Concepts*. Cambridge: MIT Press.

Pitcher, G. 1964. *Truth*. Englewood Cliffs: Prentice-Hall.

Post, J. 1987. *The Faces of Existence*. Ithaca: Cornell University Press.

Price, H. 1988. *Facts and the Function of Truth*. Oxford: Blackwell.

Price, H. 1992. "Metaphysical Pluralism." *Journal of Philosophy* 89, no. 8: 387–409.

Putnam, H. 1975. "The Meaning of 'Meaning'." Reprinted in *Basic Topics in Philosophy of Language*, edited by R. Harnish. Englewood Cliffs: Prentice-Hall.

Putnam, H. 1978. *Meaning and the Moral Sciences*. New York: Routledge.

Putnam, H. 1981. *Reason, Truth, and History*. Cambridge: Cambridge University Press.

Putnam, H. 1983. *Realism and Reason*. Vol. 3 of *Philosophical Papers*. Cambridge: Cambridge University Press.

Putnam, H. 1987. *The Many Faces of Realism*. La Salle: Open Court Press.

Putnam, H. 1989. *Representation and Reality*. Cambridge: MIT Press.

Putnam, H. 1990. *Realism with a Human Face*. Cambridge: Harvard University Press.

Putnam, H. 1992a. *Renewing Philosophy*. Cambridge: Harvard University Press.

Putnam, H. 1992b. "Replies." *Philosophy and Phenomenological Research* 52, no. 2: 430–441.

Putnam, H. 1994a. *Words and Life*. Cambridge: Harvard University Press.

Putnam, H. 1994b. "Sense, Nonsense, and the Senses: An Inquiry into the Powers of the Human Mind." *Journal of Philosophy* 91, no. 9: 445–515.

Quine, W. V. O. 1953. *From a Logical Point of View*. Cambridge: Harvard University Press.

Quine, W. V. O. 1960. *Word and Object*. Cambridge: MIT Press.

Quine, W. V. O. 1969. *Ontological Relativity and Other Essays*. New York: Columbia University Press.

Quine, W. V. O. 1970. *Philosophy of Logic*. Englewood Cliffs: Prentice-Hall.

Quine, W. V. O. 1976. *The Ways of Paradox and Other Essays*. Rev. ed. Cambridge: Harvard University Press.

Quine, W. V. O. 1981. *Theories and Things*. Cambridge: Harvard University Press.

Quine, W. V. O. 1990. *In Pursuit of Truth*. Cambridge: Harvard University Press.

Ramsey, F. P. 1927. "Facts and Propositions." Reprinted in *F. P. Ramsey: Philosophical Papers*, edited by D. H. Mellor. Cambridge: Cambridge University Press, 1990.

Rappaport, S. 1993. "Must a Metaphysical Relativist Be a Truth Relativist?" *Philosophia* 22: 75–86.

Rappaport, S. 1997. "Relativism and Truth: A Rejoinder to Lynch." *Philosophia* 25: 423–428.

Rescher, N. 1980. "Conceptual Schemes." In *Studies in Epistemology*, edited by P. French, T. Uehling, and H. Wettstein, Midwest Studies in Philosophy, no. 5. Minneapolis: University of Minnesota Press.

Rescher, N. 1993. *Pluralism: Against the Demand for Consensus*. Oxford: Clarendon Press.

Rosenthal, D. 1991. *The Nature of the Mind*. Oxford: Oxford University Press.

Rorty, R. 1972. "The World Well Lost." *Journal of Philosophy* 69, no. 19: 649–665.

Rorty, A. 1976. *The Identities of Persons*. Berkeley: University of California Press.

Rorty, R. 1979. *Philosophy and the Mirror of Nature*. Princeton: Princeton University Press.

Rorty, R. 1989. *Contingency, Irony, and Solidarity*. Cambridge: Cambridge University Press.

Rorty, R. 1992. "Putnam on Truth." *Philosophy and Phenomenological Research* 52, no. 2: 414–418.

Rorty, R. 1993. "Putnam and the Relativist Menace." *Journal of Philosophy* 90, no. 9: 443–461.

Russell, B. 1912. *The Problems of Philosophy*. Oxford: Oxford University Press.

Sacks, M. 1989. *The World We Found*. La Salle: Open Court Press.

Schmitt, F. 1995. *Truth: A Primer*. Boulder: Westview Press.

Searle, J. 1969. *Speech Acts: An Essay on the Philosophy of Language*. Cambridge: Cambridge University Press.

Searle, J. 1995. *The Construction of Social Reality*. New York: Free Press.

Sklar, L. 1992. *The Philosophy of Physics*. Boulder: Westview Press.

Slote, M. 1975. *Metaphysics and Essence*. New York: New York University Press.

Sosa, E. 1993a. "Putnam's Pragmatic Realism." *Journal of Philosophy* 90, no. 12: 605–626.

Sosa, E. 1993b. "Epistemology, Realism, and Truth." In Tomberlin 1993.

Strawson, P. F. 1950. "Truth." Reprinted in Pitcher 1964.

Strawson, P. F. 1959. *Individuals: An Essay in Descriptive Metaphysics*. New York: Doubleday, 1963.

Strawson, P. F. 1992. *Analysis and Metaphysics*. Oxford: Oxford University Press.

Swoyer, Chris. 1982. "True For." In *Relativism: Cognitive and Moral*, edited by M. Krausz and J. W. Meiland. Notre Dame: University of Notre Dame Press.

Tarski, A. 1944. "The Semantic Conception of Truth." In *Philosophy and Phenomenological Research* 4: 341–376.

Tomberlin, J., ed. 1993. *Language and Logic*. Philosophical Perspectives, no. 7. Atascadero: Ridgeview Publishing Co.

Van Cleve, J. 1996. "Minimal Truth Is Realist Truth." *Philosophy and Phenomenological Research* 56, no. 4: 872–879.

Van Gulick, R. 1992. "Nonreductive Materialism and the Nature of the Intertheoretical Constraint." In *Emergence or Reduction? Essays on the Prospects of Nonreductive Physicalism*, edited by A. Beckerman, H. Flohr, and J. Kim. New York: Walter de Gruyter.

Van Inwagen, P. 1990. *Material Beings*. Ithaca: Cornell University Press.

Van Inwagen, P. 1991. "Searle on Ontological Commitment." In Lepore and Van Gulick 1991.

Van Inwagen, P. 1993. *Metaphysics*. Boulder: Westview Press.

Williams, B. 1985. *Ethics and the Limits of Philosophy*. Cambridge: Harvard University Press.

Williams, C. J. F. 1976. *What Is Truth?* Cambridge: Cambridge University Press.

Williams, C. J. F. 1981. *What Is Existence?* Oxford: Oxford University Press.

Williams, M. 1986. "Do We (Epistemologists) Need a Theory of Truth?" *Philosophical Topics* 14: 223–242.

Williams, M. 1988. "Epistemological Realism and the Basis of Skepticism." *Mind* 97: 415–439.

Wittgenstein, L. 1922. *Tractatus Logico-philosophicus.* London: Routledge and Kegan Paul.

Wittgenstein, L. 1958. *Philosophical Investigations.* New York: Macmillan.

Wittgenstein, L. 1960. *The Blue and Brown Books.* 2nd ed. New York: Harper and Row.

Wittgenstein, L. 1969. *On Certainty.* Oxford: Basil Blackwell.

Wittgenstein, L. 1987. *Zettel.* Oxford: Basil Blackwell.

Wolterstorff, N. 1984. "Realism vs. Anti-realism." Reprinted in *Reality in Focus: Contemporary Readings in Metaphysics*, edited by P. Moser. Englewood Cliffs: Prentice-Hall.

Wright, C. 1992. *Truth and Objectivity.* Cambridge: Harvard University Press.

Wright, C. 1993. *Realism, Meaning, and Truth.* 2nd ed. Oxford: Basil Blackwell.

Wright, C. 1995. "Truth in Ethics." *Ratio* (new series) 8, no. 3: 210–226.

Index